D1322451

O R M L

OXFORD RESPIRATORY MEDICINE LIBRARY

Asthma

O R M L

OXFORD RESPIRATORY MEDICINE LIBRARY

Asthma

Dr Graeme P. Currie

MBChB, DCH, Pg Dip Med Ed, MRCP (UK), MD,
Consultant Respiratory Physician,
Aberdeen Royal Infirmary,
Aberdeen, UK

OXFORD
UNIVERSITY PRESS

OXFORD
UNIVERSITY PRESS

Great Clarendon Street, Oxford OX2 6DP

Oxford University Press is a department of the University of Oxford.
It furthers the University's objective of excellence in research, scholarship,
and education by publishing worldwide in

Oxford New York

Auckland Cape Town Dar es Salaam Hong Kong Karachi
Kuala Lumpur Madrid Melbourne Mexico City Nairobi
New Delhi Shanghai Taipei Toronto

With offices in

Argentina Austria Brazil Chile Czech Republic France Greece
Guatemala Hungary Italy Japan Poland Portugal Singapore
South Korea Switzerland Thailand Turkey Ukraine Vietnam

Oxford is a registered trade mark of Oxford University Press
in the UK and in certain other countries

Published in the United States
by Oxford University Press Inc., New York

First published 2008
GlaxoSmithKline edition printed 2008

British Library Cataloguing in Publication Data

Data available

Library of Congress Cataloging in Publication Data

Data available

Typeset by Newgen Imaging Systems (P) Ltd., Chennai, India
Printed in Italy
on acid-free paper by
L.E.G.O. S.p.A

ISBN 978–0–19–955115–6

10 9 8 7 6 5 4 3 2 1

Contents

Preface *vii*
Contributors *viii*
Symbols and abbreviations *ix*

1 Epidemiology, pathology and pathophysiology
   Graham S. Devereux   1

2 Clinical features and diagnosis
   Graeme P. Currie   11

3 Non-pharmacological management
   Graeme P. Currie   23

4 Pharmacological management and inhalers
   Graeme P. Currie   31

5 Acute exacerbations of asthma
   Richard Stretton and Graeme P. Currie   47

6 Occupational asthma
   Jon G. Ayres and Graeme P. Currie   59

7 Asthma in primary care
   Cathy M. Jackson   67

8 Asthma in special circumstances
   Patrick S. Fitch and Graeme P. Currie   75

9 Difficult asthma
   Claire A. Butler and Liam G. Heaney   81

10 New treatments and the future
   Graeme P. Currie   89

   Index 97

Preface

Asthma is a common chronic inflammatory condition affecting the airways and displays a varied phenotypic picture. It is increasingly recognized by healthcare workers and epidemiological studies suggest that along with other atopic diseases, its prevalence is rising. The precise aetiology of asthma remains uncertain, but genetic and environmental factors such as viruses, country of origin, allergen exposure, early use of antibiotics, and numbers of siblings have all been implicated in its inception and development. Pathologically it is characterized by inflammation, physiologically by airway hyperresponsiveness (or hyperreactivity) resulting in reversible airflow obstruction, and clinically by wheeze, chest tightness, breathlessness and cough. It can present in early childhood as well as adulthood, and varies markedly in severity, clinical course, subsequent disability and response to treatment. Exacerbations and symptoms of asthma are the final manifestation of a complex interplay between an array of inflammatory cells and mediators, which cause airway smooth muscle to intermittently relax and contract.

Despite greater knowledge surrounding the immunopathological origins of asthma and considerable advances in its management, it remains one of the most important chronic diseases in young Western adults and poses a significant degree of morbidity throughout all age groups. A minority of patients have difficult to control asthma and often pose significant therapeutic difficulties in specialist clinics. Exacerbations of asthma contribute to significant costs for healthcare systems and are implicated in adversely affecting the quality of life of individuals and their families. Moreover, although asthma deaths have decreased over the past few decades, an appreciable number of deaths still occur each year. Regular anti-inflammatory therapy with inhaled corticosteroids is required in all but the mildest of disease and attenuates underlying airway inflammation and hyperresponsiveness, while bronchodilators are designed to relax airway smooth muscle and prevent bronchoconstriction on exposure to bronchoconstrictor stimuli. Other forms of treatment are required in individuals with persistent symptoms and exacerbations. In recent years several potentially exciting treatments have emerged and are in varying degrees of pre-clinical and clinical development. The aim of this book is to offer a compact, practical and referenced, evidence-based guide by which to offer the reader a useful update of the main clinical aspects of the overall syndrome of asthma.

Contributors

Jon G. Ayres
BSc (Hons), MBBS, MD,FRCP,
FRCPE, FFOM
Consultant Physician,
Department of Environmental
and Occupational Medicine,
University of Aberdeen,
Aberdeen, UK

Claire A. Butler
MBChB, MRCP
Specialist Registrar in
Respiratory Medicine,
Belfast City Hospital,
Belfast, UK

Graeme P. Currie
MBChB, DCH, Pg Dip Med Ed,
MRCP (UK), MD
Consultant Respiratory
Physician, Aberdeen
Royal Infirmary,
Aberdeen, UK

Graham S. Devereux
BM BCH, MA, MD, PhD,
FRCP(Ed)
Clinical Senior Lecturer,
Honorary Consultant Physician,
Department of Environmental
and Occupational Medicine,
University of Aberdeen,
Aberdeen, UK

Patrick S. Fitch
MBChB, FRCP, MD
Consultant Respiratory
Physician, Aberdeen Royal
Infirmary, Aberdeen, UK

Liam G. Heaney
MBChB, MRCP, MD
Consultant Respiratory
Physician, Belfast City
Hospital, Belfast, UK

Cathy M. Jackson
BSc (Hons), MBChB,
MRCGP, MD
Clinical Senior Lecturer,
Community Health Sciences,
University of Dundee,
Dundee, UK

Richard Stretton
BMedSci (Hons), MBChB,
MRCP (UK)
Specialist Registrar in
Respiratory Medicine,
Freeman Hospital,
Newcastle, UK

Symbols and abbreviations

ACE	angiotensin converting enzyme
BTS/SIGN	British Thoracic Society/Scottish Intercollegiate Guidelines Network
COPD	chronic obstructive pulmonary disease
COSHH	Control of Substances Hazardous to Health
DEXA	dual energy x-ray absorptiometry
DPI	dry powder inhaler
FEV_1	forced expiratory volume in 1 second
FLAP	5-lipoxygenase activating protein
FVC	forced vital capacity
GOAL	Gaining Optimal Asthma Control
GORD	gastro-oesophageal reflux disease
HADS	Hospital Anxiety and Depression Scale
HRCT	high-resolution computerised tomography
5-HPETE	5-hydroxyperoxyeicosatetraenoic
ICAM-1	intercellular adhesion molecule-1
ICD10	International Classification of Disease-10
Ig	immunoglobulin
IL	interleukin
IV	intravenous
LABA	long acting β_2 agonist
NIV	non-invasive ventilation
NHS	National Health Service
NSAID	non-steroidal anti-inflammatory drug
pANCA	p anti-neutrophil cytoplasmic antibody
PC	provocative concentration
PD	provocative dose
PEF	peak expiratory flow
pMDI	pressurized metered dose inhaler
QOF	Quality and Outcomes Framework
RADS	reactive airways dysfunction syndrome

RAST	radioallergosorbent test
RIDDOR	Reporting of Injuries, Diseases and Dangerous Occurrences Regulations
Th	T-helper
TNFα	tumour necrosis factor alpha

Chapter 1

Epidemiology, pathology and pathophysiology

Graham S. Devereux

Key points

- Asthma is more common in affluent Westernized countries and its prevalence has increased over the last 40 years.
- Features associated with a Westernized lifestyle such as allergen exposure, hygiene, obesity and diet have been suggested as possible causes of the rise in allergic diseases such as asthma.
- Asthma is more prevalent in children (10–15%) than adults (5–10%); in children, it is more common in males, and in adults more common in females.
- A genetic tendency along with environmental influences leads to hallmark features of asthma, which are inflammation, airway hyperresponsiveness and reversible airflow obstruction.

1.1 Definition

Although asthma has been described in literature since antiquity, the condition effectively remains undefined since there are no clear-cut criteria to decide whether an individual has asthma or not. However, a 1992 International Consensus Report described asthma as:

> a chronic inflammatory disorder of the airways in which many cells play a role, in particular mast cells and eosinophils. In susceptible individuals, this inflammation causes symptoms which are usually associated with widespread but variable airflow obstruction that is often reversible either spontaneously or with treatment and causes an associated increase in airway responsiveness to a variety of stimuli.

The absence of specific defining criteria limits the interpretation of epidemiological and pathophysiological studies, which have used a range of methods to identify subjects with asthma. Studies that have used a clinical diagnosis of asthma to identify subjects are liable to subtle important inconsistencies due to variation in access, provision and quality of healthcare services and international differences in the diagnostic practices of doctors (that are also liable to change over time).

1.2 Epidemiology

1.2.1 Geographical differences

International surveys that have used standardized methodologies demonstrate marked geographical variation in the prevalence of asthma and asthma symptoms both within and between countries. In general, it is more common in the English-speaking countries of the world and less common in Eastern Europe, rural Africa, India and China. A 20-fold difference in the prevalence of asthma symptoms in the previous year in children aged 13–14 years has been reported between countries of high prevalence (25–35%), such as the UK, Australia and New Zealand, and countries with a low prevalence (≤5%) such as Eastern Europe, China, India and Ethiopia. Similarly, in young adults aged 20–44 years, diagnosed asthma is more common (5–10%) in English-speaking countries.

It is generally accepted that asthma is associated with a Westernized affluent lifestyle, with prevalence being higher in developed countries. In less well developed areas such as Africa, the prevalence among rural African children living a traditional lifestyle in the 1970s was very low when compared to urban children. However, recent studies indicate that this rural/urban gap – while still present – has narrowed appreciably and has been attributed to an increasing tendency for rural communities to adopt a more Westernized lifestyle. Migration studies suggest that the Westernized affluent lifestyle is a potent asthmagenic environment with immigrants from low prevalence areas rapidly acquiring the same susceptibility to asthma as the local population, especially if migration occurs at an early age.

1.2.2 Age and sex differences

Asthma is more common in children than adults, although of these, between 30% and 80% of children become asymptomatic around the time of puberty. However, longitudinal cohort studies suggest complex and somewhat unpredictable associations between child-hood asthma and asthma status during adult life. About a quarter of children continue to have the condition as adults and about a quarter of children who undergo remission during puberty relapse as adults. Furthermore, about 10% of children who have never wheezed will develop wheezing as adults. In childhood, asthma is more prevalent in males, but during puberty the sex ratio reverses such that asthma is more common in females. There is some evidence to suggest a further reversal of the sex ratio after the age of 50 years when asthma is probably more common in males.

1.2.3 Temporal trends

There is convincing evidence that the prevalence of asthma has markedly increased in Westernized countries since the early 1960s. While this may in part reflect the increasing awareness of family doctors of asthma, repeated cross-sectional surveys consistently report increases in wheezing illness and objective parameters of asthma such as airway hyperresponsiveness. Some of the recent increases may be secondary to the increases in atopic disease (atopic eczema, allergic rhinitis) that are recognized risk factors for the development of asthma (Figure 1.1); however there are some reports suggesting that the increase may be, to some extent, independent of the increase in atopic disease. The increase in asthma and atopic disease has been reflected in serial cross-sectional surveys of school-children aged 9–12 years in Aberdeen, where the lifetime prevalence of asthma increased from 4.1% in 1964 to 25.9% in 2004 (Figure 1.2). Reassuringly, there are now epidemiological studies suggesting that in some countries the increase in asthma may be at an end, with prevalence rates reaching a plateau or even in decline.

1.2.4 Impact of asthma

In Westernized countries, asthma is now a major public health concern due to the fact that it is a common condition which is associated with significant ill health and high societal and healthcare costs. In the UK, 10–15% of children and 5–10% of adults have been diagnosed with asthma and it has been estimated that 5.2 million individuals receive

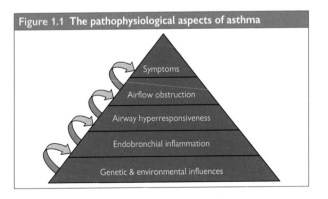

Figure 1.1 The pathophysiological aspects of asthma

Symptoms

Airflow obstruction

Airway hyperresponsiveness

Endobronchial inflammation

Genetic & environmental influences

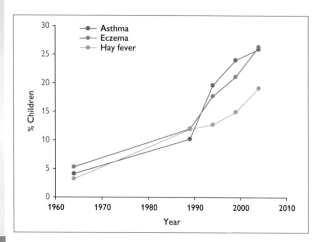

Figure 1.2 Lifetime parentally reported prevalence of asthma, eczema and hay fever in five cross-sectional surveys of Aberdeen school children aged 9–12 years between 1964 and 2004.

treatment for asthma, of whom 1.1 million are children. However, despite the large numbers of affected individuals, the mortality rate is low; around 1400 deaths were attributed to asthma in the UK in 2002, with more than two-thirds being aged 65 years or older.

Asthma is associated with significant morbidity with an estimated 2.1 million adults and 500,000 children experiencing frequent severe symptoms, while one in six individuals experience weekly attacks such that they have difficulty speaking. Moreover, 6% of asthmatics require emergency treatment every month. Individuals with asthma are significant consumers of NHS resources and services, particularly in primary care. In the UK in 2000, there were more than 18,000 first new episodes presenting to general practitioners, and there are over 4 million consultations with general practitioners annually. In 2002 there were 69,000 admissions to hospital in the UK because of asthma; admission rates for adults have remained stable over the past few years. The annual UK economic cost of asthma in 2001 was estimated to be £2.3 billion, with the 12.7 million working days that were lost annually accounting for £1.2 billion in lost productivity. A further £260 million was accounted for by social security benefits and NHS expenditure on asthma was estimated to be £889 million (Figure 1.3). In the United States, 21.3 million adults and 8.9 million children have been diagnosed with asthma at some point and 14.4 million adults and 4.0 million children have active disease. In 1994, asthma was estimated to cost the US economy $10.7 billion with $6.1 billion in direct medical costs.

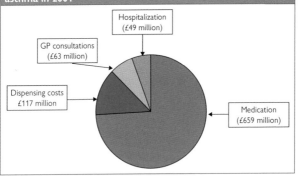

Figure 1.3 **UK National health service expenditure on asthma in 2001**

Hospitalization
(£49 million)

GP consultations
(£63 million)

Dispensing costs
£117 million

Medication
(£659 million)

1.3 Pathology

There is little doubt that asthma is an inflammatory condition of the airways. Post-mortem studies demonstrate that the lungs of individuals who have died from asthma are hyperinflated with widespread plugging of small, medium and, to some extent, large airways by thick tenacious mucus; there are also small areas of pulmonary atelectasis/collapse. The development of fibreoptic bronchoscopy with histological analysis of bronchial biopsies and cytological examination of bronchoalveolar lavage samples, has demonstrated that even mild asthma is associated with airway inflammation, albeit less severe than that observed in fatal disease.

Microscopically, asthma is associated with epithelial disruption with the shedding of epithelial cells into the airway lumen; clusters of epithelial cells form Creola bodies that can be identified in the sputum. Further characteristic features of asthmatic airways are homogeneous thickening of the subepithelial reticular basement membrane and an increase in smooth muscle mass as a consequence of hypertrophy and/or proliferation (Figure 1.4). Asthmatic airways tend to be inflamed and oedematous, and have dilated blood vessels, endothelial swelling and angiogenesis. Characteristically there is a marked cellular infiltrate of CD4+ T-helper (Th) lymphocytes of the Th2 phenotype, eosinophils and mast cells. Asthma is also associated with increased mucus production due to goblet cell hyperplasia and submucosal mucus gland hypertrophy. The excess of mucus, when mixed with inflammatory exudate, inflammatory cells and epithelial cells, form

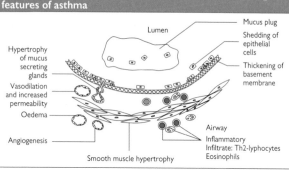

Figure 1.4 Schematic representation of the histopathological features of asthma

Lumen

Mucus plug

Shedding of epithelial cells

Hypertrophy of mucus secreting glands

Thickening of basement membrane

Vasodilation and increased permeability

Oedema

Angiogenesis

Airway Inflammatory Infiltrate: Th2-lyphocytes Eosinophils

Smooth muscle hypertrophy

highly tenacious mucus plugs that are difficult to clear and contribute to airflow obstruction. The airway lumen is further compromised by the airway thickening associated with airway inflammation and the dynamic airflow obstruction resulting from contraction of the increased airway smooth muscle mass.

1.4 Pathophysiology

1.4.1 Lymphocytes

A major advance in the understanding of the immunopathology of asthma was the demonstration that CD4+ Th cells could be categorized into two broad functional groups (Th1 and Th2) based on their secreted cytokines. Asthma and allergic disease are associated with the Th2 phenotype characterized by the secretion of interleukin (IL) 4, IL-5, IL-6, IL-9, IL-10 and IL-13 (Figure 1.5). The Th2 cytokine IL-4 induces the isotype switching of B cells to the synthesis of IgE, and IL-5 promotes the growth, differentiation and release of eosinophils from bone marrow. Other actions of Th2 cytokines include the growth, differentiation and release of mast cells from bone marrow, the localization and activation of eosinophils, and inhibition of Th1 differentiation. Th2 biased Th cells induce a package of biological responses that are characteristic of asthma, allergy and helminth infection, namely high levels of circulating immunoglobulin E (IgE), mastocytosis and tissue eosinophilia.

1.4.2 Eosinophils

Eosinophils are probably the major effector cells in asthma, with elevated numbers found in the sputum, airways and blood. Circulating eosinophils localize to inflamed airways by various adhesion molecules (such as intercellular adhesion molecule 1 (ICAM-1)) and chemokines (such as eotaxin) released by Th2 cells and inflammatory cells. Once

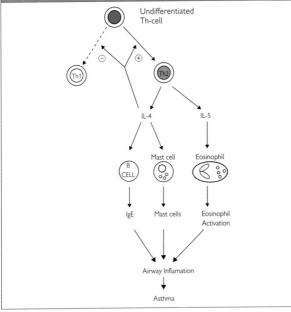

Figure 1.5 Schematic representation of Th2 cell involvement in asthma

Undifferentiated Th-cell

Th1

Th2

IL-4

IL-5

B CELL

Mast cell

Eosinophil

IgE

Mast cells

Eosinophil Activation

Airway Inflamation

Asthma

localized to the airways, activated eosinophils release highly toxic granule proteins (e.g. eosinophil cationic protein and major basic protein) and free radicals that can kill parasites, but in the inappropriate setting of asthma cause tissue damage. The synthesis and release of inflammatory molecules such as prostaglandins, leukotrienes and cytokines amplify and perpetuate the inflammatory response by further recruitment of eosinophils and lymphocytes.

1.4.3 **Immunoglobulin E**

Elevated IgE levels are a feature of atopic/allergic asthma and IgE mediates allergen-induced bronchoconstriction. The IgE stimulated by Th2 biased responses is specific for the stimulating antigen (pollens, animal or insect dander) and most is bound to tissue mast cells, which possess high affinity FcεR1 receptors on their cell surface. Exposure of IgE-coated mast cells to specific multivalent antigen induces mast cell activation by cross-linkage of the IgE molecules. Mast cell activation induces the rapid (within seconds) release of preformed (histamine, tryptase, chymase) and rapidly synthesized mediators (prostaglandins, leukotrienes). These inflammatory mediators induce bronchoconstriction, mucus secretion, vasodilatation, nerve stimulation, increased vascular permeability, tissue oedema and eosinophil chemotaxis. Activated mast cells also secrete cytokines and chemokines that promote Th2 differentiation and the influx of lymphocytes and eosinophils. Allergen-induced, IgE-mediated mast cell activation induces a characteristic rapid inflammatory response known as the immediate hypersensitivity reaction. The immediate response is rapid and intense, but short lived because of rapid degradation of the inflammatory mediators. In some individuals, the immediate response is followed 4–8 hours later by a slowly developing, intense and sustained response, known as the late phase reaction. The sustained late phase response is often considered to be the pathophysiological basis for the chronic allergic inflammatory state found in asthma. The late phase response is initiated by the mast cell degranulation of the immediate hypersensitivity reaction, which releases inflammatory mediators that recruit and activate eosinophils, neutrophils, basophils, macrophages and Th2, which release further inflammatory mediators that induce the late phase response (Figure 1.6). Once the inflammatory state has been established in asthma, the airways demonstrate an increased propensity to constrict in response to non-allergenic stimuli such as exercise, cold air and pollution. This is known as bronchial hyperresponsiveness or hyperreactivity and is believed to be the mechanism behind spontaneous and induced variability of airflow obstruction.

1.4.4 **Remodelling of airways**

Asthma is associated with structural changes of the airways (thickened basement membrane, smooth muscle hypertrophy), and in an important subgroup of individuals with asthma there is an accelerated decline in ventilatory function. This phenomenon of airway remodelling has conventionally been thought to be a consequence of chronic airway inflammation. However, there is emerging evidence suggesting that airway remodelling is an independent parallel process fundamental to asthma. The shedding of epithelial cells is a characteristic feature of asthma and normally the integrity of the surface epithelium is rapidly restored; however there is evidence to suggest that in asthma this proliferative repair response is suppressed. It has been suggested that the defective repair of airway epithelium stimulates the persistent activation and secretion of inflammatory epithelial-derived cytokines and growth factors that drive chronic inflammation and the remodelling of the subepithelial compartment.

1.5 **Genetic factors**

A well established clinical observation is that asthma and allergic disease run in families and that, in an individual, the presence of one

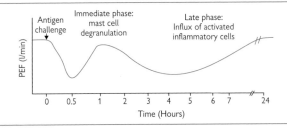

Figure 1.6 Graphical representation of an allergen challenge on airway calibre (peak expiratory flow, PEF) in an individual sensitized to the allergen. Note the immediate and late phase responses

of these conditions increases the likelihood of related conditions. Formal investigations have confirmed this clinical observation and twin studies suggest that 50–60% of asthma is inherited. In recent years the advances in molecular genetics have led to a surge in research, with over 500 studies examining polymorphisms in over 200 genes for associations with asthma and allergy. Many associations have been reported between polymorphisms in genes encoding for molecules implicated in the immunopathogenesis of asthma and allergy. For example, polymorphisms in the gene encoding the β-chain of the high affinity IgE receptor have been associated with asthma and bronchial hyperresponsiveness. Other studies have demonstrated associations between polymorphisms in the genes encoding IL-4, the α-chain of the IL-4 receptor, and IL-13. A number of associations have recently been reported for genes that are expressed on airway epithelial and smooth muscle cells (ADAM33, GPRA), and have led to the concept of airway remodelling being an independent process fundamental in the pathogenesis of asthma.

1.6 Why has the prevalence of asthma increased?

Although genetic susceptibility is a major risk factor for the development of asthma, genetic susceptibility cannot account for the recent increase in asthma that has taken place within the timespan of one generation. It is generally agreed that changing environmental factors associated with Westernization and affluence underlie the recent trend. Several features associated with such a Westernized lifestyle (allergen exposure, hygiene, obesity and diet) have been suggested as hypothetical causes of the rise in allergic disease.

1.6.1 Allergens

Allergen exposure and IgE sensitization to allergens are central to the understanding of the immunopathogenesis of asthma, while sensitization to perennial allergens such as house dust mite is associated with an increased likelihood of asthma. However, the majority of well designed intervention studies suggest that allergen avoidance does not reduce the likelihood of childhood asthma.

1.6.2 Hygiene

The hygiene hypothesis suggests that reduced exposure to a wide range of micro-organisms because of improved hygiene, cleanliness and widespread antibiotic use, may be implicated in the development of asthma. Studies of children born and brought up on farms suggesting that they are less likely to develop asthma, have focused attention on the possible beneficial effects of childhood exposure to microbial structural molecules such as endotoxin in the prevention of asthma and allergy.

1.6.3 Obesity and inactivity

It has been suggested that increasing childhood obesity and inactivity inhibits the natural growth of airways during childhood, in turn predisposing to asthma.

1.6.4 Diet

Many studies have demonstrated associations between asthma and dietary intake of antioxidants (vitamin C, vitamin E, β-carotene, selenium), polyunsaturated fatty acids (n-3, n-6) and some foodstuffs (apples, fruit juice, butter, margarine). However, dietary supplementation in adults is not associated with any clinically beneficial effect. A number of recent studies have highlighted the potentially important role of maternal diet during pregnancy in influencing the likelihood of childhood asthma, in particular, the consumption of vitamin E, vitamin D, zinc, n-3 polyunsaturated fatty acids and apples. Further studies are required before firm recommendations can be made.

Further reading

Asthma UK. (2004). *Where Do We Stand?* http://www.asthma.org.uk/document.rm?id=18 (accessed 1/6/07).

Crane J, von Mutius E, Custovic A. (2006). Epidemiology of allergic disease. In: *Allergy*, 3rd edn (eds Holgate ST, Church MK, Litchenstein LM), pp. 233–246. Elsevier St. Louis.

International consensus report on diagnosis and treatment of asthma (1992). National Heart, Lung, and Blood Institute, National Institutes of Health, Bethesda, Maryland 20892. Publication No. 92–3091, March 1992. *Eur Respir J*, **5**: 601–41.

Devereux G. (2006). The increase in the prevalence of asthma and allergy: food for thought. *Nature Rev Immunol* **6**: 869–74.

Jeffrey PK. (2001). Remodelling in asthma and chronic obstructive lung disease. *Am J Respir Crit Care Med*, **164**: S28–S38.

Ober C, Hoffjan S. (2006). Asthma genetics 2006: the long and winding road to gene discovery. *Genes Immun* **7**: 95–100.

Chapter 2

Clinical features and diagnosis

Graeme P. Currie

Key points

- Asthma is a clinical diagnosis and based around the presence of typical symptoms (intermittent cough, wheeze, breathlessness, chest tightness) and demonstration of reversible airflow obstruction.
- Reversible airflow obstruction is present if there is at least:
  - 20% variability in peak expiratory flow over 3 consecutive days;
  - 15% (plus 200 ml) improvement in forced expiratory volume in 1 second, 20 minutes after 400 micrograms of inhaled salbutamol (or 2.5 mg nebulized salbutamol) or 2 weeks of 30 mg/day of prednisolone.
- Consider an alternative (or concomitant) diagnosis if unusual features are present in the history, reversible airflow obstruction is not present, there is a poor response to treatment, or if symptoms are disproportional to abnormalities in objective measurements.

2.1 Diagnosis and clinical features

Making the diagnosis of asthma is not always straightforward. Unlike many other conditions in medicine, the diagnosis is usually based on typical features in the history often with no discriminatory examination, radiological or laboratory findings. However, it is important to identify key features in the history, perform a careful physical examination, and ideally demonstrate reversible airflow obstruction.

2.1.1 Symptoms and differential diagnosis

Classic features of asthma include wheeze, chest tightness, breathlessness, reduced exercise tolerance and cough. However, these symptoms are neither sensitive nor specific and can occur in many other pulmonary and non-pulmonary conditions. Examples of disorders that can mimic symptoms of asthma and cause diagnostic uncertainty include:

- chronic obstructive pulmonary disease (COPD)
- hyperventilation
- angiotensin converting enzyme (ACE) inhibitor induced cough
- vocal cord dysfunction
- bronchiectasis
- cystic fibrosis
- interstitial lung disease
- pulmonary thromboembolism
- lung cancer
- upper airway obstruction (e.g. vocal cord palsy, cancer, tracheomalacia, tracheal stenosis)
- pulmonary oedema
- breathlessness due to obesity or anaemia

COPD is often the main condition in the differential diagnosis of asthma in adults, and distinguishing between either condition is not always straightforward (Table 2.1). Clinicians should, however, endeavour to do so, as both conditions generally have different treatments and prognosis. In cigarette smokers, there is sometimes a degree of overlap between pure asthma and pure COPD.

Other characteristic features of asthma include symptoms which are variable, intermittent, and worse overnight or early in the morning. They are often provoked by identifiable bronchoconstrictor stimuli, although in many individuals it is not possible to discover what triggers symptoms. Examples of provoking stimuli include:

- exercise
- cold air
- respiratory infections
- cigarette smoke

Table 2.1 Clinical features that help distinguish asthma from chronic obstructive pulmonary disease (COPD)

	Asthma	COPD
Age	Any age	>35 years
Cough	Often non-productive	Frequently productive
Breathlessness	Episodic	Persistent and progressive
Atopic disorders	Common	Possible
Family history	Frequent	No link
Smoking history	Possible	Almost invariable
Lung function	Often normal	Always abnormal

- stress and anxiety
- pets and furry animals
- grass, weed and tree pollens
- drugs, e.g. β-blockers (including eye drops), non-steroidal anti-inflammatory drugs (NSAIDs) and aspirin
- food additives, e.g. tartrazine, benzoates
- environmental and occupational agents

Twin and familial studies suggest a genetic link in asthma and it is important to discover if other family members are affected. Other atopic diseases commonly coexist with asthma and clinicians should therefore enquire about a personal history of allergic rhinitis and eczema. Indeed, allergic rhinitis is found to some extent in many patients with allergic asthma; many studies have demonstrated that patients who have been treated for allergic rhinitis experience fewer exacerbations of asthma. This in turn highlights the importance of asking about symptoms such as nasal obstruction and discharge, post-nasal drip, impaired smell, chronic cough and repeated throat clearing–all of which could be consistent with allergic rhinitis– especially in patients with poorly controlled asthma.

2.2 Signs

All patients in whom the diagnosis of asthma is suspected should be examined. The examination is often completely normal but it is important to identify features that may indicate a concomitant or alternative diagnosis. Evidence of allergic rhinitis or eczema may also be found in a proportion of individuals. Patients may only have demonstrable signs–such as wheeze–during an exacerbation or following exposure to a particular trigger due to the variable nature of the condition.

2.3 Objective measures in the diagnosis of asthma

Demonstration of reversible airflow obstruction is important but not a prerequisite to the diagnosis of asthma. For example, a patient with normal lung function may only have demonstrable airflow obstruction present when exposed to a bronchoconstrictor stimulus. The demonstration of reversible airflow obstruction is often a necessity for clinical drug trials evaluating asthma treatment. However, in 'real life', it is often not possible to demonstrate a significant degree of airflow obstruction–especially in very mild asthmatics–so this should not preclude the initiation of treatment.

2.3.1 Variability in peak expiratory flow

Peak expiratory flow (PEF) is a measure of the maximal rate of exhalation. In normal adults, it peaks at the age of 30 and varies according to height, sex and age. If the PEF is normal when a patient has symptoms, then it is less likely that asthma is present. To correctly use a peak flow meter (Figure 2.1), the following steps should be followed:

• set the pointer to zero
• inhale to total lung capacity
• seal the lips around the mouthpiece
• exhale as hard and fast as possible
• record the number next to the pointer

The PEF should be taken first thing in the morning, last thing in the evening, and sometimes in between these times; the best of three attempts should be recorded into a peak flow diary. A 20% difference in PEF recordings during three consecutive days during a week over a 2-week period is usually regarded as being highly suggestive of asthma (Box 2.1).

Box 2.1 How to calculate the percentage variability

Variability = (best PEF–lowest PEF) / best PEF x 100

For example,

• Highest PEF = 500 L/min
• Lowest PEF = 400 L/min
• Variation in PEF = 500 L/min–400 L/min = 100 L/min
• % PEF variability = (500–400)/500 x 100 = 20%

2.3.2 Reversibility of peak expiratory flow

An alternative to recording a daily PEF chart is to perform a reversibility test to either β_2-agonists or corticosteroids (Figure 2.2). The PEF is recorded initially and then 20 minutes following a short-acting β_2-agonist delivered via a nebulizer (2.5 mg salbutamol) or hand-held inhaler (200 micrograms or 2 puffs of salbutamol). Alternatively, patients may be given a trial of oral corticosteroid (such as prednisolone 30 mg daily for 2 weeks). In each of these methods, an improvement in PEF of 20% from baseline and of at least 60 l/min is regarded as diagnostic of asthma.

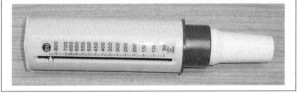

Figure 2.1 Peak expiratory flow meter

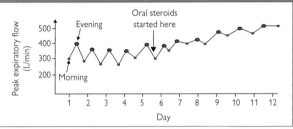

Figure 2.2 Peak expiratory flow chart demonstrating classical diurnal variability before and after treatment with oral corticosteroids

2.3.3 **Exercise testing**

Many patients–typically those with normal lung function–do not demonstrate significant reversibility following an inhaled acting β_2-agonist or course of oral prednisolone. In these patients an exercise test may be performed. PEF is measured at rest and the patient asked to exercise, for example run for 6 minutes. The PEF is then recorded every 10 minutes for 30 minutes; a fall of 20% is considered consistent with the diagnosis.

2.4 **Spirometry**

Spirometry is a forced respiratory manoeuvre, which measures forced expiratory volume in 1 second (FEV_1), forced vital capacity (FVC) and the FEV_1/FVC ratio (Figure 2.3). Due to the variable nature of asthma, spirometry may be normal. Table 2.2 shows the typical spirometric features of asthma, COPD and restrictive ventilatory defects. In more severe asthma, the FVC may become impaired, which may indicate the development of more fixed airways.

Table 2.2 Typical spirometric findings in asthma, chronic obstructive pulmonary disease (COPD) and restrictive ventilatory defects. Examples of restrictive ventilatory defects include respiratory muscle weakness, kyphoscoliosis and interstitial lung disease

	Asthma	COPD	Restrictive ventilatory defects
FEV$_1$	Normal but can be reduced	Always reduced	Reduced
FVC	Usually normal but can be reduced in advanced disease	Can be reduced or normal	Reduced
FEV$_1$/FVC	Normal or reduced	Always reduced	Normal or increased

FVC = Forced vital capacity
FEV$_1$ = Forced expiratory volume in 1 second

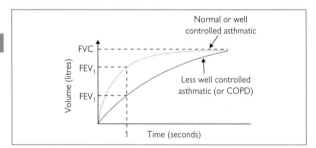

Figure 2.3 Volume–time curves showing typical features in (a) normal individuals and most well-controlled asthmatics, and (b) airflow obstruction (such as poorly controlled asthma or COPD).

2.5 Bronchial challenge testing

Bronchial challenge tests can be used to assess the extent of airway hyperresponsiveness in asthma but are not routinely used in its diagnosis. The most commonly agents used are methacholine and histamine, both of which act directly upon receptors in bronchial smooth muscle and cause contraction leading to bronchoconstriction. However, inhalation of such stimuli can also cause bronchoconstriction in non-asthmatic individuals, those with COPD and smokers. Broncho-provocation with indirect stimuli such as adenosine monophosphate, mannitol and hypertonic saline—which cause the initial release of proinflammatory mediators—are more closely associated with underlying inflammation than direct stimuli.

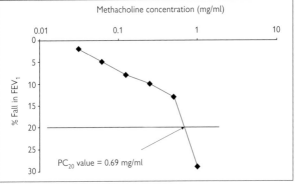

Figure 2.4 Calculation of the methacholine PC_{20} from interpolation of the $\log_{10}$ dose–response curve

Methacholine concentration (mg/ml)

% Fall in FEV$_1$

PC_{20} value = 0.69 mg/ml

Most methods of assessing the degree of airway hyperresponsiveness follow the same general principles. An initial FEV$_1$ baseline is measured prior to administration of a bronchoconstrictor stimulus. Bronchoprovocation is then carried out using doubling doses or concentrations of the stimulus. At regular intervals (usually several minutes), the best of several FEV$_1$ measurements is recorded. The test is usually terminated after a predetermined fall in FEV$_1$ is achieved (usually a 20% fall). Construction of a log dose–response curve is followed by linear interpolation, allowing the provocative dose or concentration of stimulant to be calculated. The provocative dose or concentration of agent causing a 20% fall in FEV$_1$ is usually abbreviated to PD_{20} or PC_{20} (Figure 2.4). Patients can be given a short-acting β_2-agonist to quicken their return to pre-test value or allowed to recover spontaneously. Guidelines have suggested stratifying the degree of airway hyperresponsiveness to methacholine according to the PC_{20} value (Table 2.3). Bronchial challenge tests tend to be reserved for research purposes in specialized centres, but may also be of value when diagnosis is difficult or uncertain. Patients who fail to demonstrate airway hyperresponsiveness despite significant symptoms should have the diagnosis of asthma reconsidered.

Table 2.3 **Severity of airway hyperresponsiveness according to the methacholine PC$_{20}$**	
Extent of airway hyperresponsiveness	Methacholine PC$_{20}$
Absent	>16 mg/ml
Borderline	4–16 mg/ml
Mild	1–4 mg/ml
Moderate to severe	<1 mg/ml

2.6 **Inflammatory biomarkers**

Inflammatory biomarkers such as sputum eosinophilia (Figure 2.5), exhaled nitric oxide and serum eosinophilic cationic protein are of increasing interest in determining the presence and extent of airway inflammation. Titrating asthma therapy according to lung function and surrogate inflammatory biomarkers may lead to a more superior control of asthma symptoms than using lung function alone. However, inflammatory biomarkers such as these are not widely available in everyday clinical practice for either diagnosis or tailoring management.

2.7 **Other investigations**

A chest radiograph may be required if an alternative diagnosis is considered or if patients have atypical symptoms or signs. A full blood count may also be useful, looking for the presence of a raised eosinophil count which is in keeping with the diagnosis of asthma. Skin prick tests or a radioallergosorbent test (RAST) may also be performed to identify whether individuals are sensitive to specific allergens, while an increased immunoglobulin E (IgE) level indicates that the individual is atopic.

2.8 **Asthma subtypes and associated syndromes**

2.8.1 **Allergic rhinitis**

Allergic rhinitis is a common inflammatory condition of the upper airway characterized by sneezing, nasal pruritus, rhinorrhoea and nasal obstruction. Since the upper and lower airways have a direct anatomical connection, share similar epithelial lining, and release similar inflammatory mediators, it has been suggested that asthma and allergic rhinitis represent a continuation of the same inflammatory disease process.

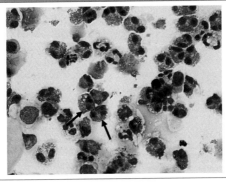

Figure 2.5 Sputum eosinophilia (see arrows) in a patient with uncontrolled asthma

Around 20–40% of individuals with allergic rhinitis are thought to have concomitant asthma, while 30–90% of asthmatics are thought to have allergic rhinitis. Uncontrolled allergic rhinitis is known to precipitate and exacerbate asthma, with the inference that clinicians should positively search for typical nasal and ocular symptoms. Moreover, successful treatment of allergic rhinitis can confer benefits in overall asthma control. Recent guidelines have emphasized the importance of identifying symptoms of asthma in individuals with rhinitis and vice versa. Current management strategies consist of allergen avoidance, immunotherapy, nasal corticosteroids and systemic or topical antihistamines.

2.8.2 Cough variant asthma

Asthma is one of the most common causes of chronic cough in non-smoking adults with a normal chest radiograph and not using an ACE inhibitor; the other main causes include post-nasal drip syndrome and gastro-oesophageal reflux. In cough variant asthma, cough tends to be the predominant symptom, especially overnight and on exertion. In such individuals, lung function may be completely normal but airway hyperresponsiveness is present. The cough usually responds well to inhaled corticosteroids.

2.8.3 Eosinophilic bronchitis

This is another condition that commonly causes chronic cough. Sputum eosinophilia is present, although typically there is no airway hyperresponsiveness, lung function is normal and no variability is present. It usually responds to inhaled corticosteroids.

2.8.4 **Aspirin-sensitive asthma**

The prevalence of aspirin-sensitive asthma is uncertain although it may exist to some extent in up to 20% of all asthmatics. Aspirin-sensitive asthma constitutes part of a syndrome where individuals demonstrate bronchoconstriction and mucosal inflammation on exposure to aspirin and other NSAIDs. Other features include nasal polyposis, rhinitis and sometimes abdominal pain. The precise pathogenesis remains unclear, but aspirin and NSAIDs selectively inhibit cyclo-oxygenase-1, which in turn shunts arachidonic acid down the 5-lipoxygenase pathway, causing overproduction of cysteinyl leukotrienes. This has given rise to the suggestion that leukotriene receptor antagonists may play a role in the management of aspirin-sensitive patients.

2.8.5 **Brittle asthma**

Two main clinical types of patients with brittle asthma have been described. Type I brittle asthmatics demonstrate a large and chaotic variability in PEF despite appropriate treatment. The variability has been expressed as >40% diurnal variation in PEF for >50% of the time over >150 days. Type II patients appear to have well-controlled asthma but develop unheralded severe episodes frequently requiring hospital admission. Management in both types is often difficult and affected individuals are at a greater risk of experiencing a life-threatening episode.

2.8.6 **Churg–Strauss syndrome**

This is a small vessel multisystem vasculitis that requires prompt recognition and appropriate management. It is a rare syndrome and is found in association with moderate to severe asthma. Other typical features include sinusitis, an eosinophil count of $>1.5 \times 10^9$/L, pulmonary infiltrates, sinus disease, signs of a systemic vasculitis and high serum IgE. Organ involvement is variable and it can affect the skin (purpura), nervous system (peripheral neuropathy or mononeuritis multiplex), cardiovascular system (pericarditis and heart failure), kidneys (renal failure) and gastrointestinal system (abdominal pain and bleeding). Other features such as fever, weight loss and malaise are often found. Tissue diagnosis is preferable and serum p anti-neutrophil cytoplasmic antibody (pANCA) is positive in about 70% of cases. Treatment consists of high dose oral corticosteroids in conjunction with immunosuppressive therapy such as cyclophosphamide. The features of systemic vasculitis are often masked by patients maintained on high dose inhaled corticosteroids. As a result, drugs that permit a lower dose of corticosteroids, such as leukotriene receptor antagonists, have been implicated (probably incorrectly) in its development.

2.8.7 Allergic bronchopulmonary aspergillosis

This condition is caused by an immunological reaction to the fungus *Aspergillus fumigatus*. The inhalation of spores causes the appearance of eosinophilic inflammatory infiltrates in the lung. Subsequent development of fungal hyphae can cause plugging of bronchi along with bronchial wall thickening, fibrosis and bronchiectasis. Major criteria for its diagnosis are:

- a long history of asthma
- raised peripheral blood eosinophil count (0.5–1.5×10^9/L)
- fleeting chest radiographic changes such as lobar collapse (Figure 2.6) and infiltrates
- presence of aspergillus precipitins (IgG)
- positive RAST (or skin prick test) to *Aspergillus*
- total serum IgE >1000 mg/ml
- bronchiectasis

Patients often complain of non-specific malaise, a deterioration in asthma control and cough productive of dark-coloured mucous plugs. Treatment consists of high dose corticosteroids along with antifungal pharmacotherapy such as itraconazole for several months (with frequent liver function test monitoring). Measuring the total IgE level is a useful tool by which to monitor treatment success.

Figure 2.6 Right lower lobe collapse in a patient with allergic bronchopulmonary aspergillosis

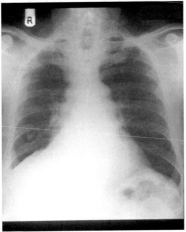

Further reading

(2004) *GINA Workshop Report, Global Strategy for Asthma Management and Prevention–updated 2004. Scientific information and recommendations for asthma programs.* NIH Publication No. 02-3659 (www.ginasthma.com).

Bousquet J, Van Cauwenberge P, Khaltaev N. (2001). Allergic rhinitis and its impact on asthma. *J Allergy Clin Immunol* **108**: S147–S334.

British Thoracic Society/Scottish Intercollegiate Guideline Network. (2003). British guideline on the management of asthma. *Thorax* **58** (Suppl 1): i1–i94.

Walker S, Sheikh A. (2005). Self reported rhinitis is a significant problem for patients with asthma. *Prim Care Respir J* **14**: 83–7.

Chapter 3

Non-pharmacological management

Graeme P. Currie

> **Key points**
> - Information about asthma (verbal and written material) at a level suitable to the individual is a vital component in management.
> - All asthmatics should have a written, personalized action plan.
> - Dietary manipulation, complementary techniques and homeopathic treatments have little or no evidence-based value in the routine management of asthma.
> - Smoking cessation should be encouraged in all asthmatics; a combination of behavourial strategies, nicotine replacement therapy or bupropion can be tried.

International guidelines have suggested the following overall goals of asthma management:

- prevention of troublesome symptoms of asthma during the day and night
- prevention of exacerbations
- maintenance of normal activity levels
- maintenance of normal or near normal lung function
- provision of optimal pharmacotherapy while minimizing the risk of adverse effects
- satisfaction with the package of care provided

Once symptoms have developed, treatment is usually indicated. This can vary from intermittent use of short-acting β_2-agonists to combinations of oral and inhaled regimes. However, several different non-pharmacological strategies are also important in achieving these aims.

3.1 **Asthma education programmes**

Sitting alongside appropriate pharmacological treatment, asthma education programmes are one of the other main features that can contribute to its overall successful management. Such programmes should consist of:

• written information and verbal education
• ability and knowledge on how to self-monitor
• regular medical reviews
• provision of an asthma action plan

In other words, all individuals should have some understanding about their condition and be given the opportunity to find out more, be encouraged to regularly monitor disease control by way of symptoms and/or peak expiratory flow (PEF), and be regularly assessed by appropriately trained nursing or medical staff. Personalized, written asthma action plans also play a vital role in most asthma education programmes. Moreover, every contact with a healthcare provider–whether in primary or secondary care–facilitates an opportunity to emphasize the importance of individuals being in control of their disease, give further education, assess inhaler technique, and where necessary alter treatment.

3.2 **Asthma action plans**

Exacerbations of asthma can occur in a variety of clinical settings. Some patients experience a deterioration over a couple of days or weeks, while others develop increased symptoms upon a background of long-standing poorly controlled asthma. Written asthma action plans tailored to the individual provide patients with an ability to detect when asthma is becoming less well controlled and indicate what should be done about it.

Personalized asthma action plans have consistently been shown to reduce hospital admissions and attendance at accident and emergency departments. Since every individual with asthma has the potential to develop airflow obstruction, it follows that self-management plans should be incorporated into everyday routine care. Despite their documented benefit, they remain a widely under-used tool in the overall care of patients. It is important to be aware that written asthma action plans do not suit every individual. For example, some patients may require different thresholds of intervention, others may have a very individualized pharmacological regime, and those with long-standing asthma may have relatively fixed airways and little variability in PEF. However, most asthma action plans should follow a similar layout and should advise:

- when to alter asthma therapy
- what to do when asthma becomes less well controlled
- how long intervention should last
- when to seek medical advice

3.2.1 When to alter asthma therapy

Patients can be advised to alter their therapy on the basis of PEF, symptoms or both. Both methods are considered to be equally effective. It is important to be aware that a reduction in PEF should be in relation to the individual's personal best, rather than on expected values calculated from a nomogram. This is of particular importance in those who have never achieved (or never will achieve) a predicted value or those with more fixed airflow obstruction. Table 3.1 shows a suggested relationship between PEF and symptoms according to stage of asthma control, although the clinician should be aware that modifications are often required to suit individual patients. For example, the threshold for intervention with patients with more severe asthma or previous life-threatening episodes may be lowered.

3.2.2 What to do and how long to do it

Current guidelines suggest that in the first instance patients should double their inhaled corticosteroid dose as the initial step when their asthma becomes less well controlled. There is no ideal length of time that such treatment should be continued, but doing so for several weeks or until symptoms have resolved is considered reasonable.

25

Table 3.1 Relationship between steps in asthma control according to peak expiratory flow (PEF) and symptoms and suggested management plans

Step	PEF	Symptoms	Management plan
1	80–100% predicted	Minimal or none	Continue with current treatment
2	60–80% predicted	Increased symptoms on exercise, at night or during a chest infection	Increase dose of inhaled corticosteroids
3	40–60% predicted	Symptoms as above plus increased short-acting β_2-agonist use with minimal relief	Start oral corticosteroids
4	<40% predicted	Marked symptoms, difficulty breathing	Refer to hospital

It should be noted that in some severe asthmatics who are already receiving high dose inhaled corticosteroids, it might be reasonable to consider starting oral corticosteroids as the first line step in their asthma action plan. Despite being based on sound theoretical reasoning, there is little evidence that increasing the inhaled corticosteroid dose outside the context of written asthma action plans is of any great benefit. However, it may well be that doing so encourages compliance and emphasizes to the patient the necessity of anti-inflammatory therapy. In patients with increased symptoms with little relief from short-acting β_2-agonists, oral corticosteroids should be commenced. Those with more severe symptoms should call for emergency advice or be taken to hospital as oral corticosteroids and regular inhaled bronchodilators in conjunction with a period of observation might be necessary.

3.2.3 **Allergen avoidance**

The majority (but not all) of individuals with asthma display an atopic tendency. Moreover, atopic sensitization to aeroallergens may increase the likelihood of developing asthma and is associated with airway hyperresponsiveness to both direct and indirect bronchoconstrictor stimuli in those with established disease. Allergen avoidance is commonly advocated in patients with asthma, especially in those who demonstrate type 1 hypersensitivity to common aeroallergens such as house dust mite, feathers, cats and dogs. However, there are a paucity of convincing evidence-based data substantiating the effectiveness of this approach in managing asthma. For example, in a double-blind, randomized, placebo controlled study involving 1122 individuals, the effects of house dust mite avoidance with the use of allergen-impermeable bed coverings was evaluated in terms of asthma control. Although the majority of patients in both groups were sensitized to house dust mite, avoidance was not associated with beneficial effects in lung function or other measures of asthma control. A Cochrane review has also indicated that there is little firm evidence to suggest that house dust mite avoidance measures definitely improve parameters of asthma control.

It is possible that with more complex and expensive interventions combining aeroallergen avoidance with other measures such as behavioural adaptation and environmental intervention where triggers are kept to a minimum, some benefits may occur. Similarly, there is little documented evidence to suggest that the removal of family pets such as cats or dogs is of benefit; however, such measures may well have some impact upon improving asthma symptoms in some highly atopic individuals.

3.2.4 Dietary intervention

All overweight patients with asthma should be advised to lose weight. This is for general health reasons and also aims to limit the degree of obesity-related breathlessness, which may be difficult to disentangle from that due to concomitant asthma. There is little convincing evidence to indicate that vitamin or mineral supplementation confers any overall significant benefit in the management of established asthma.

3.2.5 Complementary techniques

The Buteyko technique was developed in Russia and is a method by which individuals are encouraged to control their rate of breathing on the assumption that symptoms are due to hyperventilation and hypocapnia. Some data have suggested that it may confer some benefit in reducing breathlessness and the need for reliever treatment, but fails to influence other parameters of asthma control such as lung function. Guidelines do not advocate its use as standard treatment in the management of asthma, although it may be of some use in individuals in whom hyperventilation is a problem. There is also insufficient randomized controlled evidence to suggest that homeopathy, acupuncture or herbal preparations confer any benefit and are therefore not advised under normal circumstances.

3.2.6 Smoking cessation

Smoking cessation should underpin the management of all asthmatics who continue to smoke cigarettes. Not only is this important in reducing exacerbations and the prevention of smoking-related diseases, but there is also accumulating evidence that cigarette smoking reduces the efficacy of inhaled corticosteroids. Moreover, maternal cigarette smoking is often associated with wheeze in infants and young children. Individuals can be encouraged to stop smoking by a combination of behavioural strategies, nicotine replacement therapy and other pharmacological aids.

3.2.6.1 Behavioural support

All health professionals should encourage smokers to quit at every available opportunity; advice should be offered in an encouraging, non-judgemental and empathetic manner. It should be explained that cessation is not easy and that several attempts may be required to achieve long-term success. The following behavioural strategies may be of some use in helping individuals to succeed:

- support a quit attempt as soon as possible, aim for total abstinence and set a date
- review previous attempts and reflect on what has helped and what has not
- ensure that friends and colleagues are aware that a quit attempt is planned
- get rid of all cigarettes
- introduce the notion that a cigarette is a killer
- explain that cigarette smoking confers pleasure mainly because it simply prevents withdrawal symptoms
- list harmful chemicals and carcinogens that are found in cigarettes
- list diseases that cigarette smoking causes
- discuss potential nicotine withdrawal symptoms and explain that most will pass within about a month
- encourage patients to create goals and rewards for themselves
- devise coping mechanisms to use during periods of craving
- encourage partners to quit at the same time and offer them support
- make use of follow-up support
- use nicotine replacement therapy or bupropion

3.2.6.2 Nicotine replacement therapy

Nicotine replacement therapy is the most commonly used adjunct in smoking cessation therapy and increases the chances of quitting by about 1.7-fold. It acts by replacing the supply of nicotine to the smoker without delivery of toxic components.

Although some forms of nicotine replacement therapy (gum, inhalator, nasal spray, lozenges) deliver nicotine more quickly than others (transdermal patches), all deliver a lower total dose, and deliver it to the brain more slowly than a cigarette. Since there is no clear evidence that any one formulation is of greater or lesser efficacy, the best approach is to follow the preference of the individual in terms of choice of product. However, in heavy smokers, the combination of a sustained release product (in order to provide continuous background nicotine) plus a more rapidly acting product for periods of craving may be of benefit. In some individuals with relative contraindications (such as acute cardiovascular disease or pregnancy) it may be prudent to use lower doses of relatively short-acting preparations. Light smokers (less than 10 cigarettes per day), or those who wait longer than an hour before their first cigarette of the day, may also be better advised to use a short-acting product in advance of their regular cigarettes or at times of craving. Treatment is generally recommended for up to 3 months, which should be followed by a gradual withdrawal. Nicotine replacement therapy is generally well tolerated, although important prescribing points are shown in Box 3.1.

Box 3.1 Important prescribing points with nicotine replacement therapy

Adverse effects

- Nausea
- Headache
- Unpleasant taste
- Hiccoughs and indigestion
- Sore throat
- Nose bleeds
- Palpitations
- Dizziness
- Insomnia
- Nasal irritation (spray)

Cautions

- Hyperthyroidism
- Diabetes mellitus
- Renal and hepatic impairment
- Gastritis and peptic ulcer disease
- Peripheral vascular disease
- Skin disorders (patches)
- Avoid nasal spray when driving or operating machinery (sneezing, watering eyes)
- Severe cardiovascular disease (arrhythmias, post-myocardial infarction)
- Recent stroke
- Pregnancy
- Breastfeeding

3.2.6.3 *Bupropion*

Bupropion is of similar efficacy as nicotine replacement therapy in terms of smoking cessation rates. It is an antidepressant, although its beneficial effect upon smoking cessation is independent of this. Bupropion also helps to prevent the weight gain that is commonly associated with cessation. The main adverse effect is its association with convulsions and is therefore contraindicated in smokers with a past history of epilepsy and seizures. Bupropion should usually not be prescribed in individuals with risk factors for seizures; prescribers should also note that some drugs—such as antidepressants, antimalarials, antipsychotics, quinolones and theophylline—can lower the seizure threshold. Other important prescribing points are listed in Box 3.2. Unlike nicotine replacement therapy (which is usually started at the

Box 3.2 **Contraindications to prescribing bupropion**

- History of seizures
- Use of drugs that lower the seizure threshold
- Alcohol or benzodiazepine withdrawal
- Eating disorders
- Bipolar illness
- Central nervous system tumours
- Pregnancy and breastfeeding
- Hepatic cirrhosis

same time as smoking cessation), bupropion should start 1 or 2 weeks prior to the quit attempt. It should be discontinued if abstinence is not achieved within 8 weeks. There is no clear evidence that combining bupropion with nicotine replacement therapy confers any further advantage in quit rates.

Further reading

Cooper S, Oborne J, Newton S, et al. (2003). Effect of two breathing exercises (Buteyko and pranayama) in asthma: a randomised controlled trial. *Thorax* **58**: 674–9.

Gibson PG, Powell H. (2004). Written action plans for asthma: an evidence-based review of the key components. *Thorax* **59**: 94–9.

Gøtzsche PC, Johansen HK, Schmidt LM, Burr ML. (2004). House dust mite control measures for asthma. *Cochrane Database of Systematic Reviews*, 2004: CD001187.

Morgan WJ, Crain EF, Gruchalla RS, et al. (2004). Results of a home-based environmental intervention among urban children with asthma. *N Engl J Med* **351**: 1068–80.

Srivastava PS, Currie GP, Britton J. (2006). ABC of chronic obstructive pulmonary disease: smoking cessation. *Br Med J* **332**: 1324–6.

Woodcock A, Forster L, Matthews E, et al. (2003). Control of exposure to mite allergen and allergen-impermeable bed covers for adults with asthma. *N Engl J Med* **349**: 225–36.

Chapter 4

Pharmacological management and inhalers

Graeme P. Currie

Key points

- Guidelines advocate a five stepped approach to the pharmacological management of asthma in adults.
- Prior to escalating treatment, patients should have good compliance, have a satisfactory inhaler technique, and not be exposed to trigger factors wherever possible.
- Short-acting β_2-agonists should be reserved for 'as required' use in most asthmatics (step 1).
- Regular inhaled corticosteroids are required when short-acting β_2-agonists are used more than several times a week (step 2).
- The dose–response curve (in terms of lung function) for inhaled corticosteroids becomes flat at doses >800 micrograms/day of beclometasone or equivalent.
- In patients with persistent symptoms, frequent reliever use and exacerbations despite an adequate dose of inhaled corticosteroid, a long-acting β_2-agonist should be added (step 3).
- Options at step 4 consist of the addition of a leukotriene receptor antagonist, theophylline, a higher inhaled corticosteroid dose or a slow release oral β_2-agonist.
- Pharmacological treatment should usually be back-titrated following a period of clinical stability.

4.1 **Pharmacological management of asthma**

4.1.1 **Overview**

The British Thoracic Society suggests that chronic adult asthma should be managed in a stepwise fashion (Figure 4.1). Treatment can be started at any of the five steps–largely determined by the severity of symptoms–in an attempt to rapidly control symptoms. Before escalating treatment, clinicians should firstly determine that:

- the inhaler device is being used correctly
- treatment is being adhered to
- individuals are not being unnecessarily exposed to triggers

There is no reliable tool by which to assess the degree of asthma control, but it is usually done by determining:

- frequency of reliever use
- frequency of wheeze and chest tightness
- frequency of nocturnal symptoms
- limitation of activity due to symptoms of asthma
- variation in peak expiratory flow (PEF)
- forced expiratory volume in 1 second (FEV_1)
- frequency of exacerbations

Once symptoms have been stable for a 3–6-month period, therapy should usually be back-titrated in order that patients are maintained on the minimum amount of treatment that satisfactorily controls symptoms.

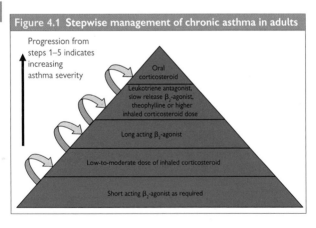

Figure 4.1 Stepwise management of chronic asthma in adults

Progression from steps 1–5 indicates increasing asthma severity

Oral corticosteroid

Leukotriene antagonist, slow release β_2-agonist, theophylline or higher inhaled corticosteroid dose

Long acting β_2-agonist

Low-to-moderate dose of inhaled corticosteroid

Short acting β_2-agonist as required

4.1.2 **Step 1: short-acting β₂-agonists**

Short-acting β_2-agonists such as salbutamol and terbutaline act directly upon bronchial smooth muscle β_2-adrenoceptors and cause the airways to dilate for up to 4–6 hours. These drugs are very quick acting, and patients can often perceive their effects within 5–10 minutes of use. All patients with asthma should be advised to use their short-acting β_2-agonist on an 'as required' basis; no benefit is conferred by regular use. There is no clear threshold at which patients should move to step 2, but it is reasonable to initiate regular anti-inflammatory therapy if patients are using their short-acting β_2-agonist more than several times a week.

4.1.3 **Step 2: inhaled corticosteroids**

Inhaled corticosteroids are a vital component in the successful treatment of persistent asthma of most severities. Once bound to cytoplasmic receptors concentrated in airway epithelial and endothelial cells, they increase and decrease the gene transcription of anti-inflammatory and proinflammatory mediators, respectively. Corticosteroids also exert a direct inhibitory effect upon a number of cells (eosinophils, T lymphocytes, epithelial cells) implicated in the asthmatic inflammatory process and attenuate airway hyperresponsiveness. Over time, they cause the airways to dilate.

Inhaled corticosteroids are the most effective first line preventer treatment in the management of asthma and, once started, should usually be used on a regular twice daily basis. The starting dose of inhaled corticosteroids should be based according to the severity of symptoms and is normally between 400 and 800 micrograms/day of beclometasone or equivalent in adults. It is important to note that fluticasone is twice as potent as beclometasone and budesonide on a microgram equivalent basis.

Dose–response studies using inhaled corticosteroids have demonstrated that most therapeutic gain is achieved with beclometasone equivalent doses up to 800 micrograms/day; at doses above this, there is an exponential increase in adverse effects with little further gain in terms of lung function (Figure 4.2). In other words, at daily doses of >800 micrograms of beclometasone or equivalent in adults, the dose–response curve for desired effects becomes flat, while that for systemic adverse effects becomes steep. However, due to the heterogeneity of asthma, it is likely that some patients do experience further benefit in asthma control with higher doses. Indeed, in patients with persistent symptoms despite using 800 micrograms/day of inhaled corticosteroid plus a long-acting β_2-agonist, one therapeutic option (step 4) is to further increase the dose of inhaled corticosteroid.

Figure 4.2 Dose–response curve effect of inhaled corticosteroids in asthma

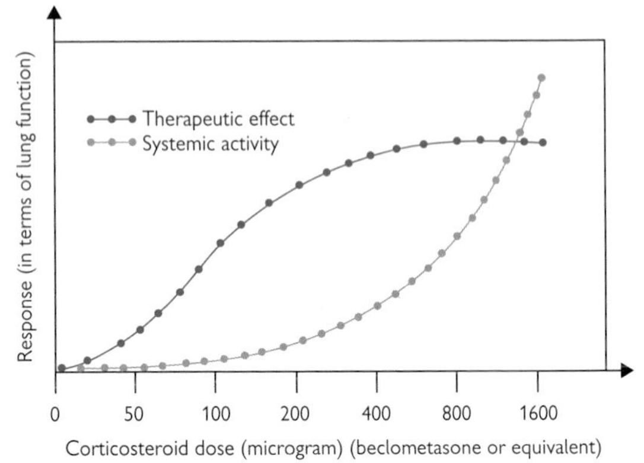

4.1.3.1 *Adverse effects*

Adverse effects of inhaled corticosteroids tend to occur in a dose-dependant way. However, at doses up to 800 micrograms/day, oral candidiasis and dysphonia (alteration in the quality of voice) are the only commonly encountered short-term adverse effects in adults. In an attempt to avoid these problems, patients should be encouraged to rinse their mouth, gargle and brush their teeth after taking their inhaled corticosteroid. Using a spacer device can also minimize these problems as they reduce oropharyngeal deposition and improve lung deposition. Some studies have shown that skin bruising occurs more commonly in patients using inhaled corticosteroids, and variable effects have been observed in the reduction of bone mineral density and suppression of the hypothalamic–pituitary–adrenal axis.

4.1.4 **Step 3: Long-acting β₂-agonists**

Salmeterol and formoterol are the most commonly prescribed long-acting β₂-agonists in clinical practice. Both bind to airway smooth muscle β₂-adrenoceptors and demonstrate a bronchodilating effect in excess of 12 hours after a single inhalation. In contrast to short-acting β₂-agonists, long-acting β₂-agonists are highly lipophilic, which partly explains their prolonged duration of action. These drugs exhibit no clinically meaningful anti-inflammatory effects and should therefore *never* be used as monotherapy. Long-acting β₂-agonists have two clinically important properties, namely a bronchodilator effect in the presence of low bronchomotor tone and a protective effect in the presence of increased bronchomotor tone.

Various studies have shown that the addition of a long-acting β₂-agonist is usually superior to doubling the dose of inhaled corticosteroid in individuals with persistent symptoms. As a consequence, in individuals who experience persistent symptoms and exacerbations despite low-to-medium doses of inhaled corticosteroid (400–800 micrograms/day of beclometasone or equivalent), guidelines advocate a therapeutic trial of long-acting β₂-agonist as add on therapy. If there is no clinical response, the long-acting β₂-agonist should be discontinued and the inhaled corticosteroid dose should be increased to 800 micrograms/day. If some response occurs, the long-acting β₂-agonist should be continued and the inhaled corticosteroid dose be increased to 800 micrograms/day (Figure 4.3). If symptoms persist thereafter, step 4 treatment should be considered.

4.1.4.1 *Adverse effects*
Long-acting β₂-agonists are usually well tolerated, but adverse effects include:

- tachycardia
- fine tremor
- headache
- muscle cramps
- prolongation of the QT interval
- hypokalaemia
- feelings of nervousness

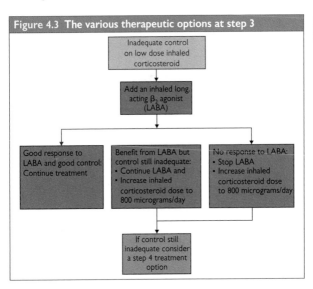

Figure 4.3 The various therapeutic options at step 3

Several recent studies have suggested that long-term use of a long-acting β_2-agonist (salmeterol) may be associated with an increase in asthma-related deaths and life-threatening events in susceptible populations such as African Americans. However, these findings may have been due to the fact that many of the individuals included in the clinical trials were using long-acting β_2-agonists as monotherapy (without regular anti-inflammatory treatment). Nevertheless, this has prompted the United States Food and Drug Administration to announce important safety information regarding inhalers containing long-acting β_2-agonists and to advise that new labelling be produced outlining the 'small but significant risk in asthma-related deaths' associated with their regular use.

4.1.4.2 *Combined inhaled corticosteroid plus long-acting* β_2-*agonist inhalers*

The use of an inhaled corticosteroid combined with a long-acting β_2-agonist in a single device is becoming an increasingly popular method of delivering drugs to the lung. Indeed, in asthmatics with persistent symptoms despite inhaled corticosteroids alone, common sense suggests that such an approach would appear to be a reasonable pharmacological option since inhaled corticosteroids are the most potent anti-inflammatory agents and long-acting β_2-agonists are the most potent bronchodilators available. Currently, salmeterol can be given with fluticasone in a single inhaler (Seretide®), and formoterol has been formulated with budesonide (Symbicort®).

Possible advantages of combination inhalers include:

- fewer inhalations
- fewer inhaler devices
- patients perceive fairly immediate bronchodilatation due to the long-acting β_2-agonist moiety
- anti-inflammatory compliance is facilitated due to the inseparable nature of the inhaler constituents
- potential synergistic action between the inhaled corticosteroids and long-acting β_2-agonists when given together
  Possible disadvantages of combination inhalers include:
- altering the inhaled corticosteroid dose (without altering the long-acting β_2-agonist dose) is less straightforward
- patients may be started on combination inhalers as first line preventer treatment rather than inhaled corticosteroids alone (in other words temptation may result in step 3 treatment being initiated when step 2 treatment would be perfectly adequate)
- relative expense
- less easy to back-titrate treatment without the provision of a separate inhaler device containing inhaled corticosteroid alone

4.1.5 Step 4: leukotriene receptor antagonists

Cysteinyl leukotrienes (C_4, D_4 and E_4)–previously known as the slow relaxing substance of anaphylaxis–are lipid mediators produced from arachidonic acid (Figure 4.4). Following synthesis, cysteinyl leukotrienes activate cell membrane receptors found on airway smooth muscle and macrophages. This results in a variety of undesirable effects in the airway such as:

- mucous hypersecretion
- hypertrophy and proliferation of smooth muscle
- bronchoconstriction
- inhibition of mucociliary clearance
- increased pulmonary vascular permeability
- recruitment of inflammatory cells
- release of acetylcholine from nerve fibres

The effects of cysteinyl leukotrienes in the airway can be influenced by inhibiting their formation (using a 5-lipoxygenase inhibitor) or by preventing binding to their receptor (using a leukotriene receptor antagonist). Zileuton is the only licensed 5-lipoxygenase inhibitor and is given four times a day. It is available for use in only some countries, and regular treatment necessitates frequent liver function tests to monitor for potential hepatotoxicity. Montelukast, zafirlukast (Figure 4.5 and Table 4.1) and pranlukast are orally active leukotriene receptor antagonists that selectively antagonize the cell surface cysteinyl leukotriene 1 receptor. These drugs confer both weak anti-inflammatory and bronchodilator effects; they also attenuate airway hyperresponsiveness.

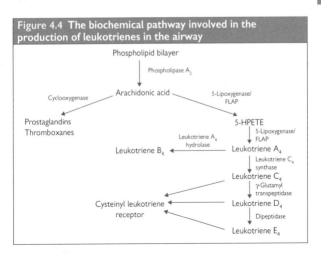

Figure 4.4 **The biochemical pathway involved in the production of leukotrienes in the airway**

Figure 4.5 The chemical structures of montelukast and zafirlukast

Zafirlukast

Montelukast

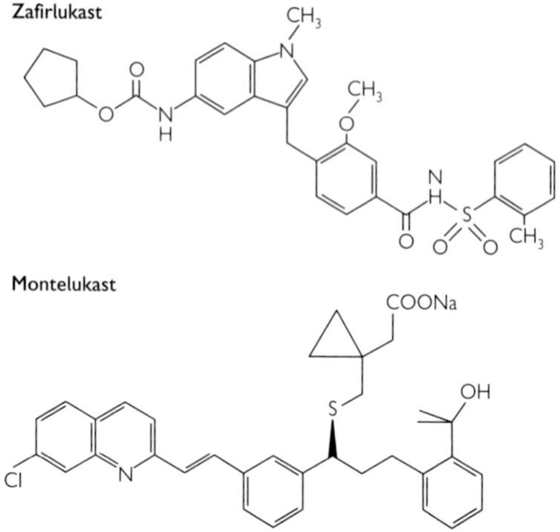

Table 4.1 Prescribing and pharmacokinetic data for montelukast and zafirlukast

Generic name	Montelukast	Zafirlukast
Brand name	Singulair®	Accolate®
Mode of action	Inhibitor of leukotriene receptor	Inhibitor of leukotriene receptor
Adult dose	10 mg daily	20 mg twice daily
Paediatric licence	Yes	No
Prescribing in renal impairment	No dose adjustment	No dose adjustment
Prescribing in hepatic impairment	No dose adjustment in mild to moderate dysfunction	Reduced clearance
Use in pregnancy	Limited data	Limited data
Protein binding	>99%	>99%
Half-life	2.7–5.5 hours	10 hours
Time to peak levels	3–4 hours	3 hours
Bioavailability	64%	Uncertain
Special instructions	Can be taken with food	Avoid with food
Interaction with warfarin	Not known to interact	Increases prothrombin time

Current guidelines suggest that a leukotriene receptor antagonist should be considered when either the combination of an inhaled corticosteroid plus long-acting β_2-agonist fails to satisfactorily control symptoms, or following a failed trial of long-acting β_2-agonist (step 4). Leukotriene receptor antagonists may also have some use in:

- patients with both asthma and allergic rhinitis
- exercise-induced asthma
- aspirin-induced asthma
- asthmatics who are unable or unwilling to use inhaler devices

4.1.5.1 *Adverse effects*

Leukotriene receptor antagonists are generally well tolerated. However, adverse effects such as hypersensitivity reactions, arthralgia, pulmonary eosinophilia, gastrointestinal disturbances, sleep disorders, respiratory infections, hallucinations, seizures and raised liver enzymes have been reported. In the UK, leukotriene receptor antagonists are not advised in pregnancy unless absolutely essential. Concern has been raised regarding the development of Churg–Strauss syndrome and administration of leukotriene receptor antagonists, although many of the documented cases have occurred where concomitant leukotriene receptor antagonist has allowed a reduction in inhaled corticosteroid dose. This in turn suggests that latent Churg–Strauss syndrome may have been unmasked by a decrease in anti-inflammatory therapy delivered to the lungs.

4.1.6 **Step 4: theophylline**

Theophylline is a phosphodiesterase inhibitor and demonstrates activity in a multitude of cell types throughout the body. It also has a variety of other effects such as increased interleukin-10 release, enhanced apoptosis, inflammatory mediator inhibition and increased catecholamine release. Although it has only modest clinical efficacy in asthma, theophylline is orally active and relatively inexpensive, in turn making it an attractive therapeutic option, especially in less wealthy populations. When used in asthma, these drugs confer weak bronchodilator and anti-inflammatory action effects. Current guidelines suggest that a therapeutic trial of theophylline can be considered in patients with persistent symptoms despite a low-to-moderate dose of inhaled corticosteroid plus long-acting β_2-agonist (step 4). Theophylline should initially be started at a low to moderate dose and the plasma concentration checked before titrating the dose upwards, or when adding in a new drug which may alter its metabolism. Target levels are between 10 and 20 mg/L (55–110 μM). At theophylline concentrations greater than this, the frequency of adverse effects tends to increase to unacceptable levels.

4.1.6.1 *Adverse effects*

The use of theophylline is frequently limited due to concerns of cardiac arrhythmias, gastrointestinal upset, and the need for monitoring plasma levels due to a narrow therapeutic index. Moreover, there is considerable variation in the half-life of theophylline and care needs to be taken in certain medical conditions and when using particular drugs that alter its half-life and plasma clearance.

Causes of increased plasma theophylline levels (i.e. reduced plasma clearance) include:

- heart failure
- liver cirrhosis
- advanced age
- ciprofloxacin
- erythromycin
- clarithromycin
- verapamil

Causes of reduced plasma theophylline levels (i.e. increased plasma clearance) include:

- cigarette smokers
- chronic alcoholism
- rifampicin
- phenytoin
- carbamazepine
- lithium

4.1.7 **Step 5: oral corticosteroids**

Long-term use of oral corticosteroids (usually prednisolone) should be avoided if at all possible, although if absolutely necessary, the lowest possible dose that controls symptoms should be used. In the most severe asthmatics who require high doses of oral corticosteroids for prolonged periods of time, immunosuppressants may be occasionally tried under expert supervision. Patients who are to receive long-term oral corticosteroids should be aware that they should not be stopped suddenly and that a slow reduction in dose is usually necessary. Immediate withdrawal after prolonged administration may lead to acute adrenal insufficiency and even death; all patients receiving oral corticosteroids should be given a treatment card alerting others on the problems associated with abrupt discontinuation. Courses of oral corticosteroids that last less than 3 weeks do not normally require to be tapered before stopping.

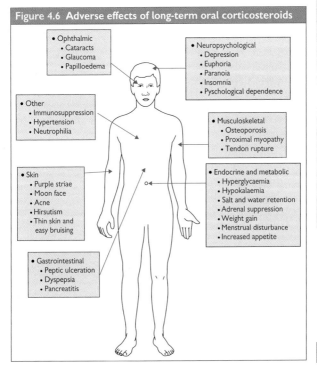

Figure 4.6 Adverse effects of long-term oral corticosteroids

- Ophthalmic
  - Cataracts
  - Glaucoma
  - Papilloedema

- Neuropsychological
  - Depression
  - Euphoria
  - Paranoia
  - Insomnia
  - Pyschological dependence

- Other
  - Immunosuppression
  - Hypertension
  - Neutrophilia

- Musculoskeletal
  - Osteoporosis
  - Proximal myopathy
  - Tendon rupture

- Skin
  - Purple striae
  - Moon face
  - Acne
  - Hirsutism
  - Thin skin and easy bruising

- Endocrine and metabolic
  - Hyperglycaemia
  - Hypokalaemia
  - Salt and water retention
  - Adrenal suppression
  - Weight gain
  - Menstrual disturbance
  - Increased appetite

- Gastrointestinal
  - Peptic ulceration
  - Dyspepsia
  - Pancreatitis

4.1.7.1 *Adverse effects*

The risk of corticosteroid-induced osteoporosis is related to cumulative dose. This implies that in addition to individuals on maintenance prednisolone, those requiring frequent courses may experience long-term complications. Patients using at least 7.5 mg/day of prednisolone (or equivalent) for 3 months are at heightened risk of adverse effects along with those over the age of 65 years. Prolonged use of oral corticosteroids can be associated with a variety of other undesirable adverse effects. Examples of these are shown in Figure 4.6.

4.2 Inhalers

Inhalers are used by most patients to facilitate the delivery of anti-inflammatory and bronchodilator therapy to the endobronchial tree. Unfortunately with all inhalers a substantial proportion of the drug is deposited in the oropharynx (Figure 4.7). Some groups of patients, for example children or the elderly, have difficulty in using inhaler devices and oral asthma therapy may be required. Prior to the introduction of inhaled therapy, it is crucial that patients are instructed on how to use the device correctly and are comfortable with the particular device. Assessment of inhaler technique should be carried out at every available opportunity.

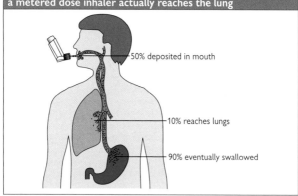

Figure 4.7 Only a small proportion of the drug emitted from a metered dose inhaler actually reaches the lung

50% deposited in mouth

10% reaches lungs

90% eventually swallowed

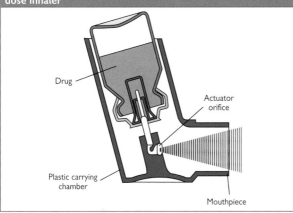

Figure 4.8 A diagrammatic representation of a metered dose inhaler

Drug

Actuator orifice

Plastic carrying chamber

Mouthpiece

One of the most common inhaler devices is a pressurized metered dose inhaler (pMDI; Figure 4.8). To use a pMDI correctly, patients should be asked to:

- shake the canister
- take a full breath out (i.e. exhale to residual volume)
- put their lips around the mouthpiece
- press *only once* with the inhaler in the mouth and at the same time suck inwards quickly (to total lung capacity)
- hold their breath for up to 10 seconds
- breathe out normally

Patients notoriously find it difficult to use pMDIs, though many other inhaler types are available. This has resulted in a bewildering array of different types of inhalers available for use. However, in general, whichever inhaler type the patient finds easy to use and feels confident in using, is a reasonable way of deciding which one is best.

4.2.1 Inhalers for adults

A pMDI plus spacer device (Figure 4.9) and dry powder inhaler (DPI) are the most effective hand-held devices providing they are used correctly. Despite being useful in delivering drugs to the lung, the main drawbacks with spacers is the fact that many individuals feel they are bulky, and less portable and convenient to use than DPIs. DPIs are designed to be breath activated, which in turn overcomes the problem of coordination (when compared to using a pMDI without a spacer). Several different types of breath-activated hand-held DPIs are available for use; commonly used types include Accuhalers™, Turbohalers® and Easi-breathe™ inhalers.

Figure 4.9 A metered dose inhaler with spacer attached

4.2.2 Use and maintenance of spacers

Some patients develop oral candidiasis and dysphonia when using a pMDI alone to deliver inhaled corticosteroids. Along with gargling, mouth rinsing and brushing teeth after using the inhaler, adding a spacer device addresses this common problem. A spacer is a large plastic container with an opening at either end; one opening to attach the inhaler and the other the mouthpiece. In general, they serve two functions. Firstly, they avoid problems in coordinating the timing of the inhaler actuation and inhalation. Secondly, they slow down the speed of delivery of the aerosol into the mouth, which minimizes the 'cold freon' effect and in turn results in less drug deposited in the oropharynx. Different manufacturers make different sizes of spacers and inhalers which should generally be used together. The following principles of use can be applied to most types:

- make sure the inhaler fits snugly into the end of the spacer device
- take a full breath out and then put the mouthpiece in your mouth
- press the inhaler once
- take a full breath inwards and hold your breath for up to 10 seconds if possible (some patients find up to 5 tidal breaths easier)
- these steps should be repeated if a second 'puff' is required
- wipe clean the mouthpiece after use
- spacers should generally be cleaned at least once a month with soapy water and be left to drip dry
- spacers should be replaced every 6–12 months, depending on the manufacturer's recommendations

4.2.3 Nebulizers

Nebulizers, driven by compressed air or oxygen, create a mist of drug particle which is inhaled by the patient via a face mask or mouthpiece. They tend to be used during an acute episode of asthma, either in the primary or secondary care setting. Some patients with more severe asthma use a nebulizer on a domiciliary basis although objective benefit should generally be a prerequisite. However, it is important to point out that using a nebulizer is probably as effective as using a pMDI plus spacer correctly. Furthermore, despite delivering far higher doses than inhalers, nebulizers tend to be inefficient as most of the aerosol mist is lost to the atmosphere. Using a nebulizer can take as long as 10–20 minutes, while using an inhaler takes only a fraction of this time.

Further reading

(1997). BTS guidelines on current best practice for nebulizer treatment. *Thorax* **52** (Suppl 2): S1–S106.

Bateman ED, Boushey HA, Bousquet J, et al. (2004). Can guideline-defined asthma control be achieved? The Gaining Optimal Asthma Control study. *Am J Respir Crit Care Med* **170**: 836–44.

British Thoracic Society/Scottish Intercollegiate Guideline Network. (2003). British guideline on the management of asthma. *Thorax* **58** (Suppl 1): i1–i94.

Currie GP, McLaughlin K. (2006). The expanding role of leukotriene receptor antagonists in chronic asthma. *Ann Allergy Asthma Immunol* **97**: 731–42.

Shrewsbury S, Pyke S, Britton M. (2000). Meta-analysis of increased dose of inhaled corticosteroid or addition of salmeterol in symptomatic asthma (MIASMA). *Br Med J* **320**: 1368–73.

Masoli M, Weatherall M, Holt S, et al. (2005). Moderate dose inhaled corticosteroids plus salmeterol versus higher doses of inhaled corticosteroids in symptomatic asthma. *Thorax* **60**: 730–4.

Nelson HS, Weiss ST, Bleecker ER, Yancey SW, Dorinsky PM. (2006). The Salmeterol Multicenter Asthma Research Trial: a comparison of usual pharmacotherapy for asthma or usual pharmacotherapy plus salmeterol. *Chest* **129**: 15–26.

Chapter 5

Acute exacerbations of asthma

Richard Stretton and Graeme P. Currie

Key points

- A variety of behavioural and psychological traits are associated with an increased risk of dying from an episode of acute asthma.
- The main pharmacological adjuncts in the management of acute asthma consist of inhaled β_2-agonists, systemic corticosteroids and oxygen in hypoxic patients.
- Inhaled ipratropium and intravenous magnesium and aminophylline can be considered if a patient fails to respond to initial treatment.
- A rise in arterial pCO_2 or fall in pH are ominous features; individuals with these features should be urgently discussed with intensive care.

5.1 Epidemiology

There has been an overall decrease in the number of hospital visits by patients with asthma in the past 20 years. However, this is mostly in the paediatric population, with the rates of accident and emergency attendances and admission to hospital remaining much the same in the adults. In 2002 there were over 69,000 admissions to hospital in the UK due to an acute exacerbation of asthma. These admissions alone cost the NHS around £49 million, although this figure fails to include prescription costs and lost productivity due to days off work. In 2002 there were over 1400 deaths in the UK attributable to asthma, with over two-thirds of these in adults over 65 years of age. There has been a gradual decline in the number of deaths since the late 1980s, although this trend appears to be slowing. In the UK, there are more asthma deaths in younger populations in summer months, while a greater number of older individuals die in winter.

5.2 Aetiology

Exacerbations of asthma can be caused by a variety of stimuli such as viral and bacterial infections, allergens, pollutants, some drugs and occupational exposures (Table 5.1). Following all types of exposure, the end result is inflammatory cell influx and activation, exaggerated airway hyperresponsiveness, smooth muscle contraction and airflow obstruction, all of which leads to typical symptoms.

Table 5.1 Causes of exacerbations of asthma

Stimulus causing an exacerbation	Examples
Virus	Rhinovirus Respiratory syncytial virus Influenza Human metapneumovirus
Bacteria	*Mycoplasma pneumoniae* *Chlamydia pneumoniae* *Streptococcus pneumoniae*
Allergens	Pollen Cat Dog House dust mite
Environmental pollutants	Cigarette smoke (active or passive) Sulphur dioxide Nitrogen dioxide Diesel fumes Ozone Particulate matter
Drugs	Aspirin Non-steroidal anti-inflammatory drugs β-blockers (including eye drops)
Occupational exposures	See Chapter 6

5.3 Pathogenesis

A variety of inflammatory cells, cytokines and mediators take part in a complex sequence of events to produce the vasodilatation, increased mucus secretion, oedema and bronchoconstriction that leads to features of an acute exacerbation of asthma. The complexity of the reaction is increased by the fact that many of the cytokines not only promote cellular activity but also have a direct effect on the bronchial walls and vasculature. Post-mortem studies have shown that the cause of death in asthma is asphyxiation due to small airway obstruction. In such cases, a thickened and oedematous basement membrane becomes infiltrated with a variety of cell types, which produce a large amount of mucus and fibrin which is shed into the airway.

5.4 Clinical features

Patients tend to have limited perception of the severity of their asthma, which may in turn cause delay in seeking medical advice and result in clinicians underestimating the severity of an exacerbation. Moreover, many factors have been associated with an increased risk of having a fatal or near fatal episode of asthma (Box 5.1). Usual symptoms of an exacerbation are increased breathlessness, reduced exercise tolerance, cough (occasionally productive of yellow sputum), chest tightness, wheeze and increased β_2-agonist use. Some patients will have kept a record of peak expiratory flow and will therefore be able to provide objective evidence of deteriorating asthma control.

Box 5.1 Medical and psychosocial features associated with a fatal or near fatal episode of asthma

Alcohol or drug abuse
Psychiatric illness
Denial
Non-concordance with prescribed medication
Learning difficulties
Inadequate follow-up
Increased use of reliever therapy
Inadequate use of oral or inhaled corticosteroid s
Income and employment difficulties
Previous hospital self-discharge
Social isolation
Brittle asthma
Previous admission to intensive care for asthma

49

Clinical assessment is used not only to confirm the presence of an exacerbation but to assess severity, which in turn guides appropriate management (Table 5.2). The most commonly used parameters include:

- general observations such as central cyanosis, sweating, confusion and coma
- peak expiratory flow
- ability to talk in sentences
- respiratory rate
- heart rate
- blood pressure
- accessory muscle use
- chest signs
- oximetry

Table 5.2 Clinical features of moderate, severe and life-threatening exacerbations of asthma

Feature	Moderate	Severe	Life-threatening
General	Breathless but able to complete whole sentences	Sitting forward, anxious, using accessory muscles, unable to complete sentences	Exhausted, confused, unable to speak, cyanosed, comatose
Peak expiratory flow	>50% of best	33–50% of best	<33% of best
Respiratory rate	<25/min	≥25/min	Poor effort, low respiratory rate
Oxygen saturation	Usually >92%	Usually >92%	<92%
Pulse	<110/min	≥110/min	Bradycardia, arrhythmias possible
Chest signs	Expiratory wheeze	Expiratory wheeze	Silent chest

The use of pulsus paradoxus has been abandoned as it is both awkward to perform and adds little to assessment or subsequent management.

5.5 Investigations

Arterial blood gases should be performed if the oxygen saturation is <92% (whether breathing room air or oxygen) or if there is evidence of a severe or life-threatening exacerbation. In the majority of exacerbations requiring hospital admission, patients will have features of type 1 respiratory failure (Table 5.3). With clinical features of severe or life-threatening asthma, the presence of a rising pCO_2 level and falling pH (type 2 respiratory failure) is an ominous feature and highlights the need for consideration of invasive ventilatory support. Moreover, a normal pCO_2 level provides little reassurance as the increased respiratory rate during an exacerbation should result in a reduction in pCO_2. In other words, if the pCO_2 level is within the normal range during an exacerbation of asthma, it may be an early indicator that the patient is becoming tired.

A chest radiograph should be performed in patients with severe or life-threatening exacerbations, and where consolidation or pneumothorax is suspected (Figs. 5.1 and 5.2). A chest radiograph should also be considered in patients with milder disease who fail to respond quickly to treatment.

Table 5.3 Arterial blood gas features of type 1 and type 2 respiratory failure

	Type 1 respiratory failure	Type 2 respiratory failure
pO_2	↓	↓
pCO_2	↔ or ↓	↑
HCO_3	↔	↑ or ↔
pH	↔ or ↑	↔ or ↓

Figure 5.1 Chest radiograph showing a right-sided pneumothorax in a patient admitted with a concomitant exacerbation of asthma

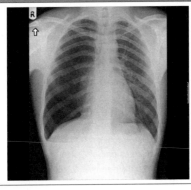

Figure 5.2 Chest radiograph showing a chest drain inserted into the right pleural cavity of the patient in Figure 5.1

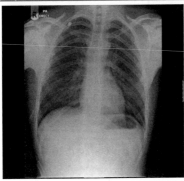

5.6 **Admission to hospital**

Up to 20% of all individuals presenting at an accident and emergency department are admitted to hospital. Individuals in the community or in the accident and emergency department who have a peak expiratory flow >75% of personal best or predicted (before or 1 hour after treatment), may be allowed home so long as treatment for the exacerbation has been provided and advice given to seek further help in the event of a deterioration. However, other individuals with peak expiratory flow >75% predicted may need to be admitted to hospital when there are concerns regarding compliance, social isolation, pregnancy, previous life-threatening episodes or persistent symptoms.

5.7 **Management**

The pivotal components of the management of acute asthma consist of inhaled bronchodilators, systemic corticosteroids and the administration of oxygen (Figure 5.3). The severity of exacerbation will determine where treatment takes place (in primary care, accident and emergency departments, specialized respiratory wards or high dependency/intensive care units).

5.7.1 **Oxygen**

Oxygen should be given to patients who have an exacerbation of asthma to maintain oxygen saturation ≥92%. Unlike chronic obstructive pulmonary disease, there is less danger of high flow oxygen causing loss of hypoxic drive and subsequent CO_2 retention. However, there is concern that injudicious administration of high flow oxygen may mask a clinical deterioration despite maintenance of an oxygen saturation of 100%; in such individuals, a fall in oxygen saturation may herald a late and ominous feature of respiratory function.

5.7.2 **Inhaled bronchodilators**

Inhaled β_2-agonists underpin the management of all individuals with an exacerbation of asthma. Although a nebulizer does not confer any additional advantage in drug delivery over hand-held devices with a spacer, they are independent of patient effort and are sometimes more convenient in the busy ward or accident and emergency setting; 400 micrograms of salbutamol via a spacer device is equivalent to 2.5 mg of salbutamol delivered via a nebulizer. Salbutamol should usually be given in repeated intervals of around 20 minutes depending on clinical response. In individuals with life-threatening asthma, continuous administration of nebulized (oxygen driven) salbutamol should

Figure 5.3 Algorithm showing the main steps involved in managing acute severe asthma in hospital

| 1. | Initial treatment |

- Oxygen to keep oxygen saturation ≥ 92%
- Salbutamol 500 micrograms (via an oxygen-driver nebulizer)
- Ipratropium bromide 500 micrograms (via an oxygen-driven nebulizer)
- Prednisolone 40 mg or IV hydrocortisone 100 mg
- Chest radiograph if pneumothorax or consolidation are suspected or patient requires intensive care

IF LIFE THREATENING FEATURES ARE PRESENT:

- Discuss with a senior doctor
- IV magnesium sulphate 2 g
- Nebulized β_2 agonist more frequently e.g. salbutamol 5 mg up to every 15–30 minutes

| 2. | Subsequent treatment |

IF PATIENT NOT IMPROVING AFTER 15–30 MINUTES:

- Nebulized β_2 agonist more frequently e.g. salbutamol 5 mg up to every 15–30 minutes
- 500 micrograms ipratropium 4–6 hourly until patient is improving

IF PATIENT IS STILL NOT IMPROVING:

- Discuss with a senior doctor
- IV magnesium sulphate 2 g *(unless already given)*
- Consider IV β_2 agonist or IV aminophylline

| 3. | Further assessment |

- Repeat PEF 15–30 minutes after starting treatment
- Maintain oxygen saturation ≥ 92%
- Repeat blood gas measurements within 2 hours of starting treatment if:
  - initial pO_2 <8 kPa (60 mmHg) unless subsequent SpO_2 >92%
  - pCO_2 normal or raised
  - patient deteriorates

Transfer to intensive care:

- Deteriorating PEF, marked hypoxia, or hypercapnia
- Exhaustion, feeble respirations, confusion or drowsiness
- Coma or repiratory arrest

be given at 5–10 mg/h. Intravenous β_2-agonists may occasionally be used when effective nebulized treatment is not possible such as in ventilated patients or those in extremis.

Ipratropium has been shown to confer additive bronchodilator effects to those achieved by inhaled β_2-agonists alone. Nebulized ipratropium (500 micrograms) should therefore be considered in patients who fail to respond to inhaled salbutamol and should be repeated after a minimum of 60 minutes; subsequent treatment should be given every 4–6 hours.

5.7.3 **Corticosteroids**

Systemic corticosteroids are a fundamental component in the management of asthma exacerbations. Prednisolone 40–50 mg should be given orally for all patients at presentation, although 100 mg of intravenous hydrocortisone may be necessary if the patient is too breathless or vomiting. Oral prednisolone is well absorbed via the enteral route and its onset of action is the same as intravenous hydrocortisone; studies have generally shown than intravenous treatment confers little advantage over oral formulations. Some data have suggested that high dose inhaled corticosteroids may be as effective as oral corticosteroids during acute exacerbations, although further trials are required to fully determine whether this should become part of standard treatment.

5.7.4 **Magnesium**

Magnesium causes relaxation of bronchial smooth muscle and subsequent bronchodilatation. It is now recommended in patients who fail to improve despite inhaled bronchodilators and systemic corticosteroids. However, a Cochrane meta-analysis of intravenous magnesium in acute asthma failed to demonstrate a beneficial effect in terms of improved lung function or reduced hospital admission rates, although some benefit was observed in those with a more severe exacerbation. In individuals presenting with a severe exacerbation, magnesium should be given as a single dose of 2 g in 50–100 ml of 0.9% NaCl over 20 minutes; serum magnesium levels do not require to be measured before or after administration.

5.7.5 **Aminophylline**

Aminophylline is a methyl xanthine and confers weak anti-inflammatory and bronchodilatory effects in asthma. In a Cochrane meta-analysis evaluating the use of intravenous aminophylline in acute asthma, active treatment failed to confer any beneficial effects although it did result in a significant increase in vomiting, palpitations and arrythmias. Despite this, guidelines suggest that it may be used in individuals with severe and life-threatening disease who respond poorly to conventional treatment. In patients not using an oral theophylline preparation, a loading dose of 5 mg/kg over at least 20 minutes should be given with cardiac monitoring with subsequent maintenance infusion of 500 micrograms/kg/h. In patients already using a theophylline preparation, the loading dose should be omitted and a plasma level should ideally be obtained prior to commencement of a maintenance infusion of 500 micrograms/kg/h. Plasma theophylline levels should be measured daily and the infusion rate altered to maintain a concentration between 10 and 20 mg/L (55–110 μmol/L).

5.7.6 **Antibiotics**

Most studies have indicated that there is no significant benefit over standard care when antibiotics are added into the routine treatment algorithm. Antibiotics should only be used when there is objective evidence of bacterial infection such as chest radiograph consolidation, systemic features of sepsis or positive microbiological culture.

5.7.7 **Leukotriene receptor antagonists**

Leukotrienes can be found in the airway and urine following both spontaneous exacerbations of asthma and acute exposure to bronchoconstrictor stimuli in the laboratory. This in turn indicates that these inflammatory mediators may have a role in the pathogenesis of acute episodes of bronchoconstriction. Although leukotriene receptor antagonists are not currently advocated in the management of acute asthma, there are data to suggest that they might be of some potential benefit. Indeed, some preliminary studies have demonstrated that leukotriene receptor antagonists do confer some benefit when given at the time of an acute exacerbation, although further large-scale studies are required to confirm these observations.

5.7.8 **Non-invasive ventilation**

Non-invasive ventilation (NIV) is useful in patients with exacerbations of chronic obstructive pulmonary disease who have decompensated hypercapnic respiratory failure. Few data are available to support its use in respiratory failure due to asthma and, as a consequence, intubation and mechanical ventilation remains the 'gold standard' approach. However, NIV may be considered in the intensive care setting under specialized supervision, providing a low threshold exists towards switching to more conventional ventilation.

5.7.9 **Invasive ventilatory support**

Patients need to be considered for referral to the intensive care unit for consideration of invasive ventilation when they fail to respond to aggressive therapy. Typical clinical features that merit transfer include exhaustion with poor respiratory effort, respiratory arrest, confusion, drowsiness, deteriorating peak expiratory flow, persisting hypoxia, hypercapnia or falling pH. Ideally the intensive care unit should be made aware of an individual with life-threatening features beforehand to allow a more smooth transition of care.

5.7.10 **Subsequent management**

Oxygen should be continued to maintain saturation at ≥92%. Oral prednisolone should usually be given for at least for 5 days (frequently 7 days) and tapering the dose is not usually required. Inhaled (usually nebulized) salbutamol should be given 4–6 hourly as well as on an 'as required' basis. Individuals should remain on their usual maintenance inhalers throughout the treatment period. Peak expiratory flow measurements should be recorded up to four times daily to assess for improvement. Intravenous fluids should be given in dehydrated patients. Consideration should be given to thromboprophylaxis with low molecular weight heparin in immobile patients and those at high risk of venous thromboembolism.

5.8 **Discharge planning**

Suitability for discharge depends on an improvement in clinical condition and varies between patients. Ideally, individuals should:

- have a peak expiratory flow >75% predicted and a diurnal variability <25%
- have regular nebulized bronchodilators discontinued 24 hours prior to anticipated discharge
- be using maintenance inhalers and provided with oral corticosteroids
- have been reviewed by an asthma nurse and provided with a written action plan
- be advised to attend their general practioner or practice nurse within 2 days of discharge and be reviewed at a respiratory clinic within 4 weeks

5.9 **Prevention**

The prevention of exacerbations is centred on the use of optimal preventer therapy and the provision of comprehensive asthma education programmes comprising general information, self-monitoring of disease activity, regular medical or nursing reviews, and an individualized, written asthma action plan. These have been discussed in Chapter 3.

Further reading

Aldington S, Beasley R. (2007). Asthma exacerbations: assessment and management of severe asthma in adults in hospital. *Thorax* **62**: 447–58.

British Thoracic Society/Scottish Intercollegiate Guideline Network. (2003). British guideline on the management of asthma. *Thorax* **58** (Suppl 1): i1–i94.

Cates CJ, Crilly JA, Rowe BH. (2006). Holding chambers (spacers) versus nebulizers for beta-agonist treatment of acute asthma. *Cochrane Database of Systematic Reviews*, Issue 2. Art. No. CD000052. DOI: 10.1002/14651858.CD000052.pub2.

Camargo CA, Jr, Smithline HA, Malice MP, Green SA, Reiss TF. (2003). A randomized controlled trial of intravenous montelukast in acute asthma. *Am J Respir Crit Care Med* **167**: 528–33.

Parameswaran K, Belda J, Rowe BH. (2000). Addition of intravenous aminophylline to beta2-agonists in adults with acute asthma. *Cochrane Database of Systematic Reviews*, Issue 4. Art. No. CD002742. DOI: 10.1002/14651858.CD002742.

Rodrigo GJ. (2006). Rapid effects of inhaled corticosteroids in acute asthma: an evidence-based evaluation. *Chest* **130**: 1301–11.

Rowe BH, Bretzlaff JA, Bourdon C, Bota GW, Camargo CA. (2000). Magnesium sulfate for treating exacerbations of acute asthma in the emergency department. *Cochrane Database of Systematic Reviews*, Issue 1. Art. No. CD001490. DOI: 10.1002/14651858.CD001490.

Chapter 6

Occupational asthma

Jon G. Ayres and Graeme P. Currie

Key points

- Occupational asthma is the cause of 10–15% of new asthma occurring in adulthood.
- The two main types of occupational asthma are classical occupational asthma (due to sensitization to a workplace exposure over time) and reactive airways dysfunction syndrome (due to a single large exposure to an agent, often following a spill).
- Two-hourly peak expiratory flow measurements provide a good way of confirming occupational asthma. Specific bronchial challenge is the final arbiter of a causal relationship although this is not routinely available.
- In addition to standard pharmacological treatment, management includes substitution of the causal agent, changes in work practice and provision of personal protective equipment. If these are ineffective or impossible, redeployment either within the same workplace or elsewhere may be necessary.

6.1 Overview

Occupational asthma, asthma caused by exposure to agents in the workplace, is more common than usually appreciated. It accounts for 10–15% of new cases of asthma arising in working age individuals. The two main types are classical sensitizing occupational asthma and reactive airways dysfunction syndrome (RADS), which is due to a single large exposure to a chemical (such as a 'spill' at work). Both types need to be differentiated from asthma aggravated by work, which is observed in those with pre-existing asthma.

6.2 Classical occupational asthma

Patients with classical occupational asthma report symptoms with a work-related pattern; improvements are observed during weekends or holidays, although in some individuals such a clear association may not be immediately obvious. Clinicians should maintain a high level of suspicion that there could be an occupational cause to asthma when encountering any newly diagnosed adult. In individuals who work in a relatively high risk occupation, such as bakers and paint sprayers, the diagnosis should be positively sought. The key questions when considering a diagnosis of occupational asthma include:

• are symptoms better at the weekends when away from work?
• are symptoms better when on holiday?

6.2.1 Causes of occupational asthma

Classical occupational asthma is caused by a sensitizing reaction in the airways in response to a specific 'asthmagen'. Occupational asthmagens (agents encountered at the workplace that cause occupational asthma) can generally be classified by molecular weight. Low molecular weight (<5000 Daltons) asthmagens largely consist of chemicals such as isocyanates, aldehydes, metals and drugs. High molecular weight (≥5000 Daltons) asthmagens are mostly proteins. Common examples of these include flour and grain dust, animal proteins (such as those found in rat urine), latex and enzymes used in baking or biological washing powders. There are currently over 400 recognized occupational asthmagens; some of the most commonly implicated agents and associated occupations are shown in Table 6.1.

Table 6.1 The most common agents known to cause classical occupational asthma in the UK and the most common occupations involved	
Agent	Occupation
Isocyanates	Paint sprayers
Flour and grain	Bakers
Cutting oils and coolants	Engineering
Paints	Wide range of industries
Chrome compounds	Electroplaters, welders
Wood dust	Timber workers
Laboratory animal proteins	Laboratory workers
Acrylics and acrylates	Building industry, chemical processes
Solder, colophony	Plumbers, engineering workers
Enzymes, amylase	Washing powder manufacture, baking

6.2.2 **Pathogenesis**

Low molecular weight asthmagens do not directly result in the production of antibodies. They work by acting as haptens, which bind onto human proteins and are usually highly reactive compounds. There are certain molecular 'structure alerts' that are much more likely to do this. Typical examples include the isocyanate moiety (–N=C=O), primary and secondary amines, dicarboxylic acid anhydrides and dialdehydes. These agents may be implicated in paint sprayers, solderers and cleaners, epoxy resin workers and hospital staff, respectively.

High molecular weight agent asthmagens usually exert their effects through an immunoglobulin (Ig) E response. The majority tend to be proteins or glycoproteins of animal or vegetable origin. In some situations the agent contains intrinsic enzymatic activity such as alcalase in occupational asthma due to detergents. As a result of their own enzymatic activity, they may potentiate allergenicity of the molecule itself by disrupting tight junctions between cells.

6.2.3 **Clinical features**

Symptoms of occupational asthma are similar to those of typical asthma in that patients commonly report wheeze, chest tightness, breathlessness and cough when exposed to the responsible agent at work. An accurate occupational history is fundamental to the correct diagnosis and should include details of all previous and current jobs, which allows assessment of exposure to known sensitizing agents. Knowledge of each job since leaving school enables both the identification of unsuspected exposures and determines the latent period prior to the development of symptoms, as most cases occur within 2 years of first exposure to the relevant agent. A pattern of symptoms being better away from work (either at the weekend or for longer periods away such as on holiday) provides the first clue that symptoms are work related. In some cases symptoms are worse in the evening after exposure, and a work-related pattern can therefore be easily missed. This is due to the late phase immunological reaction observed with some exposures. Knowledge that other individuals at the same workplace have work-related symptoms or overt occupational asthma is also helpful, although this is usually not apparent on first presentation. A possible diagnosis of occupational asthma should be investigated as soon as the possibility has arisen, as removal from the source is the most effective treatment and persistent exposure may result in irreversible symptoms.

6.2.4 **Diagnosis**

Supporting objective evidence for occupational asthma depends on demonstrating characteristic patterns of lung function variation with exposure–usually peak expiratory flow (PEF) (Figure 6.1). Occasionally, changes in forced expiratory volume in 1 second (FEV_1) across a work shift where exposure occurs is used. PEF measurements are easy to arrange, easy to perform and are cheap, but disadvantages include erratic compliance, discrepancies in the recording of accurate values and lengthy and frequent measuring periods.

To diagnose occupational asthma, the PEF should ideally be measured:

- every 2 hours from wakening to sleeping
- over 5 weeks during a period of unaltered asthma pharmacotherapy (with the exception of 'as required' use of short-acting β_2-agonists which should be recorded)
- for at least 3 days during each work period
- with at least three series of consecutive work days and three periods away from the workplace
- preferably including a 1-week period away from work

Evaluation of PEF recordings can be carried out using a computer programme (OASYS) that accurately interprets serial measurements and calculates variability in readings. However, analysis of the data by an experienced clinician remains a prerequisite in overall assessment.

Where PEF monitoring is unreliable or cannot be performed, non-specific airway hyperresponsiveness can be measured using increasing concentrations of inhaled methacholine or histamine. A greater than

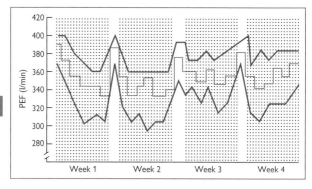

Figure 6.1 The figure shows 2 hourly peak expiratory flow (PEF) recordings in a textile worker; shaded areas represent days of exposure and clear areas time away from work. For each day, the maximum, minimum and mean PEF values are plotted. During exposure, the PEF fell and subsequently recovered when away from exposure. In the last week, although still at work, the individual was not exposed to material dust thereby explaining why the PEF recordings were relatively well maintained.

3.2-fold difference (in values when at work versus when away from work) in provocative concentration of methacholine causing a 20% fall in FEV_1 is regarded as being significant. However, it should be noted that not all individuals with occupational asthma demonstrate airway hyperresponsiveness to methacholine. When no longer exposed, airway hyperresponsiveness usually resolves over a 2–3-year period.

When doubt remains as to the true causal relationship between a suspected agent and asthma symptoms, a specific airway challenge to the suspected occupational asthmagen may be undertaken. This is generally regarded as the gold standard in the diagnosis of occupational asthma but is not widely available.

6.2.5 Management

In the work setting, the occupational physician should aim to identify responsible asthmagens and remove the worker from exposure. In some cases this will depend upon reducing exposure to a level at which sensitization or the development of asthma is unlikely to occur. However, in only a very few cases is there sufficient evidence to support a clear threshold below which sensitization will not occur. The best approach is usually to remove the particular asthmagen completely and find a substitute material to work with. When this is not possible or impractical, for instance in baking where the agent cannot be replaced, changes in work practice might be feasible with the aim of reducing exposure. As a last resort, personal protective equipment should be provided, for instance as in laboratory animal and pharmaceutical workers. If all these measures fail or are impossible, the worker may have to be relocated or move to a different job. Replacement of the relevant agent can be very effective in individual workplaces such as has been seen with the fall in latex asthma in healthcare workers with the introduction of latex- and powder-free gloves. Rates of glutaraldehyde asthma were markedly reduced by the introduction of different working practices, namely the enclosure of sterilizing units in endoscopy suites and theatres.

In the UK, the Control of Substances Hazardous to Health (COSHH) regulations mean that employers are required to document all agents that workers are exposed to and any associated risk to health. Under the Reporting of Injuries, Diseases and Dangerous Occurrences Regulations (RIDDOR) employers are also requested to report cases of occupational asthma once confirmed.

The pharmacological treatment of occupational asthma is essentially the same as that of typical asthma. This should be based on a stepwise management regime incorporating the use of intermittent short-acting β_2-agonists and regular inhaled corticosteroids with the possible addition of long-acting β_2-agonists in those with persistent symptoms.

6.2.6 **Prognosis**

If removed from exposure, the outlook is good for many individuals, but in some the condition persists despite removal from the specific cause. In some exposures (notably isocyanates), accelerated loss of lung function can occur even after removal from the cause.

Occupational asthma is costly. The main financial burden is borne equally between the patient and state, with employers bearing very little of the overall cost. The exception to this is in specific instances where major changes to the workplace are required.

6.3 **Reactive airways dysfunction syndrome**

RADS occurs generally as a consequence of a large, single exposure to gas, vapour or fumes although more diffuse sources such as the dust from the destruction of the World Trade Centre has also resulted in this condition. The commonest recorded agent causing RADS is chlorine gas.

Individuals will not have had previous respiratory symptoms (although some accept the diagnosis in patients who have had prior symptoms) and atopy is usually absent. Symptoms typically develop within 24 hours of exposure and non-specific airway hyperresponsiveness must persist for at least 3 months. Patients with RADS complain of similar symptoms to those with typical asthma, although cough is frequently a dominant feature. In RADS, spirometry may be normal or obstructive but non-specific airway hyperresponsiveness to methacholine is the cardinal feature. A diagnosis of RADS is difficult to sustain without this.

The treatment of RADS is similar to that of other forms of asthma, although patients may be significantly far less responsive to the effects of β_2-agonists and inhaled corticosteroids. The more long-term clinical outcome of RADS is poorly understood and individuals may demonstrate persistent airway hyperresponsiveness and have symptoms for many years following exposure.

6.4 **Work-aggravated asthma**

It is often difficult to distinguish true occupational asthma from individuals with previously diagnosed asthma which is aggravated by the work environment. For example, stimuli such as exercise, dust, cold air and tobacco smoke can induce or exacerbate symptoms in those with previously diagnosed asthma who would not usually be exposed to such agents when at home. This is often just as difficult a problem for the work occupational physician to deal with as classical occupational asthma. However, the aim is similar, namely to reduce the relevant exposure in order to maintain the worker's health and work efficiency.

6.5 Legal issues

In many countries, classical occupational asthma is a compensatable disease for which the government provides a pension, but this may not apply to RADS. In some cases, workers need to consider civil law approaches in order to achieve redress. Work-aggravated asthma is not compensatable.

Further reading

www.occupationalasthma.com

Newman Taylor AJ, Nicholson PJ, eds. (2004). *Guidelines for the Prevention, Identification and Management of Occupational Asthma: evidence review and recommendations*. British Occupational Health Research Foundation, London.

Rachiotis G, Savani R, Brant A, MacNeill SJ, Taylor AN, Cullinan P. (2007). Outcome of occupational asthma after cessation of exposure: a systematic review. *Thorax* **62**: 147–52.

Chapter 7

Asthma in primary care

Cathy M. Jackson

Key points

- The primary care contract recognizes that the responsibility for the diagnosis and long-term management of asthma lies principally with the primary healthcare team.
- The Quality Outcome Framework of the new primary care contract sets out seven indicators of quality of care for asthmatic patients.
- The diagnosis is usually made on the basis of typical symptoms and the demonstration of peak expiratory flow variability.
- Review should be proactive rather than reactive.

7.1 The primary care contract

The recently introduced primary care contract recognizes asthma as a common condition in which responsibility for both the diagnosis and subsequent long-term management lies principally with the primary healthcare team. Indeed, asthma is one of the most common chronic conditions diagnosed in a primary care setting and the majority of all asthmatics will be managed entirely by the primary team with secondary referral occurring in only a small minority of more challenging cases.

To ensure that the quality of care provided for all patients with asthma is optimal, it is important to have in place mechanisms for identifying these patients, ensuring regular reviews and employing staff capable of delivering current best practice to each patient. While most practices have had some form of asthma clinic in place for many years, the Quality Outcome Framework (QOF) of the new contract has necessitated that information on all patients is complete and readily accessible. This has lead to many healthcare teams reviewing and improving the consistency of delivery of care.

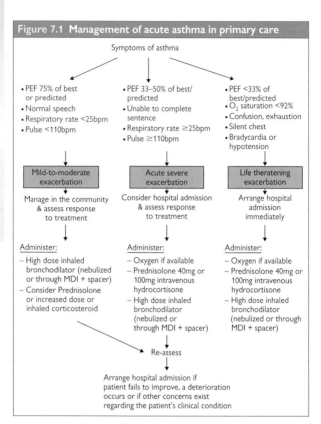

Figure 7.1 Management of acute asthma in primary care

Symptoms of asthma

- PEF 75% of best
  or predicted
- Normal speech
- Respiratory rate <25bpm
- Pulse <110bpm

- PEF 33–50% of best/
  predicted
- Unable to complete
  sentence
- Respiratory rate ≥25bpm
- Pulse ≥110bpm

- PEF <33% of
  best/predicted
- O₂ saturation <92%
- Confusion, exhaustion
- Silent chest
- Bradycardia or
  hypotension

Mild-to-moderate
exacerbation

Acute severe
exacerbation

Life theratening
exacerbation

Manage in the community
& assess response
to treatment

Consider hospital admission
& assess response
to treatment

Arrange hospital
admission
immediately

Administer:
– High dose inhaled
  bronchodilator (nebulized
  or through MDI + spacer)
– Consider Prednisolone
  or increased dose or
  inhaled corticosteroid

Administer:
– Oxygen if available
– Prednisolone 40mg or
  100mg intravenous
  hydrocortisone
– High dose inhaled
  bronchodilator
  (nebulized or
  through MDI + spacer)

Administer:
– Oxygen if available
– Prednisolone 40mg or
  100mg intravenous
  hydrocortisone
– High dose inhaled
  bronchodilator
  (nebulized or through
  MDI + spacer)

Re-assess

Arrange hospital admission if
patient fails to improve, a deterioration
occurs or if other concerns exist
regarding the patient's clinical condition

Asthma lends itself to assessment of quality of care by outcome. This is largely due to it being an area where there are widely accepted clinical guidelines and good evidence to suggest that, in the populations studied, health benefits can be achieved if there are mechanisms in place to ensure that guidelines are followed in practice. The QOF of the new primary care contract currently sets out seven indicators of quality of care of patients with asthma (Table 7.1), which in turn determines the level of payment received for provision of that care.

Table 7.1 Quality Outcome Framework suggested by the new primary care contract

Records	'The practice can produce a register of patients with asthma, excluding patients with asthma who have been prescribed no asthma-related drugs in the last 12 months'
Initial management	'The percentage of patients aged eight and over diagnosed as having asthma from 1 April 2003 where the diagnosis has been confirmed by spirometry or peak flow measurements'
Continuing management	'The percentage of patients with asthma between the ages of 14 and 19 in whom there is a record of smoking status in the previous 15 months'
Continuing management	'The percentage of patients aged 20 and over with asthma whose notes record smoking status in the past 15 months, except those who have never smoked where smoking status need be recorded only once since diagnosis'
Continuing management	'The percentage of patients with asthma who smoke, and whose notes contain a record that smoking cessation advice or referral to a specialist service, where available, has been offered within the last 15 months'
Continuing management	'The percentage of patients with asthma who have had an asthma review in the last 15 months'
Continuing management	'The percentage of patients aged 16 years and over with asthma who have had influenza immunisation in the preceding 1 September to 31 March'

This set of indicators was developed in line with the British Thoracic Society/Scottish Intercollegiate Guidelines Network (BTS/SIGN). Although it provides only a very crude measurement of the quality level for provision of care, the requirement for this information to guide the level of payment received has ensured that all practices revisit the manner in which they deliver care and where necessary, that changes are made to current practice to ensure a consistently high level of care.

7.2 Diagnosis

As asthma is most commonly diagnosed in primary care, the first step in the provision of care is the ability to diagnose it with some degree of confidence. Symptoms may vary widely between individuals, and the disease may become quiescent for long periods of time. Active inflammation of the airways can also be present without the patient being aware of any symptoms. These three factors can make both the diagnosis and management of asthma challenging at times.

The diagnosis is most frequently made on the basis of the history with supporting evidence from lung function tests (see Chapter 2). During history taking, it is important not only to consider the nature, timing and duration of symptoms but also family history, smoking, occupation, recreational activities, pets, known allergies, current medication and the presence or absence of symptoms of rhinitis and atopy.

7.3 Reasons for referral

It is occasionally necessary to refer patients for further investigations or management decisions. Patients requiring a further opinion might include those for whom there is some doubt about the diagnosis and may require further investigations, those who remain symptomatic or have frequent exacerbations despite being at step 3 on the BTS/SIGN guidelines. It is also reasonable to refer patients whose current or previous occupation may play a part in symptoms in order to accurately assess their condition and any causative agents. In acute asthma, a guide to management in primary care (and whom to refer to hospital) is shown in Figure 7.1.

7.4 Recording

Once confident of the diagnosis of asthma, patient details should be recorded in a regularly updated, and preferably electronic and password protected, disease register of all cases. This should ideally include all relevant information for ongoing management and demon-strate the level of quality outcomes achieved for remuneration purposes. The information recorded in such a database should be readily retrievable using any search enquiry, such as '>12 months since last review', not only for QOF but also for audit purposes and service planning.

7.5 **Review**

It is important that a mechanism is in place to ensure that all patients with asthma are offered the opportunity to have their condition reviewed on a regular basis with a frequency determined by need–but at least once every 12 months. Current evidence suggests that 'proactive structured review, as opposed to opportunistic or unscheduled review, is associated with reduced exacerbation rates and days lost from normal activity'. Regular review allows not only patient's symptoms, lung function tests and treatment to be assessed, but can also fulfil several other functions.

As a basic minimum, the QOF suggests that the following assessment is carried out at review appointments:

- assess symptoms using the Royal College of Physicians' three questions:
  1. In the last month have you had difficulty sleeping because of your asthma symptoms (including cough)?
  2. In the last month have you had your usual asthma symptoms during the day (cough, wheeze, chest tightness or breathlessness)?
  3. In the last month has your asthma interfered with your usual activities, e.g. housework, work/school, etc.?
- peak expiratory flow value
- inhaler technique
- ensuring that individuals have a personalized asthma plan

A review appointment facilitates an opportunity to discuss with patients any anxieties regarding asthma in general, management regimes or problems that may affect the patient's ability to take treatment as prescribed. A review appointment can also provide an opportunity for patient education in terms of self-management, lifestyle factors and vaccination. An individual, written asthma management plan should be drawn up together with the patient thereby allowing them to have a large degree of control of their own treatment in response to symptoms. Smoking status can also be checked and patients who smoke should also be assessed as to their readiness to change and interventions offered where necessary. Perhaps one of the most useful functions of a regular review appointment is to strengthen the relationship and approachability between those providing the service and the patient. This may enable queries or concerns regarding the patient's condition or treatment to be addressed *before* problems are encountered.

7.6 Staff development

Since asthma is a common chronic disorder, ongoing staff training should be a priority for all practices. Indeed, good asthma management relies on all members of the primary care team having a suitable level of knowledge and ensuring that all individuals are not only trained in current best practice but are also able to access current guidelines and have the time and facilities to be able to apply them. Training should not only involve current treatment regimes and future treatments, but also encompass those communication skills likely to improve an individual's understanding of asthma and encourage concordance with treatment plans and changes in lifestyle where appropriate. Training should apply not only to clinical staff, but also administrative staff, to enable automatic recall of patients and the recording and retrieval of data.

7.7 Limitations of QOF

At present the QOF uses only the criteria of: being able to identify asthmatics, a review with at least a solitary peak expiratory flow measurement once in 15 months, assessing smoking status, advice on cessation strategies where appropriate, and the offer of vaccinations according to current schedules. These are considered to be the very basic requirements of asthma management and aim to ensure that every practice is able to provide a streamlined care plan for every asthma patient.

One area that has not yet been addressed in the QOF indicators is determining whether or not there is any evidence of rhinitis and ensuring appropriate treatment where required. Many patients with asthma experience symptoms from concomitant rhinitis and current evidence and guidelines suggest that if upper airways inflammation is optimally treated, a commensurate improvement in asthma control will be achieved. Thus, the addition of one further indicator in the next version of asthma QOF indicators—such as the number of patients diagnosed with asthma who also have symptoms of rhinitis—might at least raise awareness in this area and provide for more efficient treatment of the unified airway.

There is at present surprisingly little evidence that monitoring symptoms, peak expiratory flow, inhaler technique and lifestyle in primary care will have any effect on the course of the disease in patients. At present, most research is performed in a secondary care setting, which represents individuals at the more severe extreme of the disease spectrum who are not truly reflective of the majority of patients with asthma. As a consequence, findings may not be confidently extrapolated into the asthma population as a whole. Moreover, one perhaps unforeseen advantage of the new QOF data is that the databases produced by practices may allow researchers to access information more easily. This, in turn, may increase the amount of evidence-based data and research produced from a primary care setting with the ultimate aim of improving the care of all asthmatic patients.

Websites

Useful websites for clinicians:
- www.brit-thoracic.org.uk (British Thoracic Society)
- www.dh.gov.uk/en/Policyandguidance/Organisationpolicy/ Primarycare/Primarycarecontracting/index.htm (accessed August 2007).
- www.gpiag.org (General Practice Airways Group)
- www.occupationalasthma.com (occupational asthma website)
- www.sign.ac.uk (Scottish Intercollegiate Guidelines Network)

Useful websites for patients:
- www.asthma.org.uk (leading UK asthma charity)
- www.allergyuk.org (UK allergy foundation)
- www.lunguk.org (leading UK lung charity)
- www.laia.ac.uk (Lung and Asthma Information Agency)

Further reading

Bousquet J, Van Cauwenberge P, Khaltaev N. (2001). Allergic rhinitis and its impact on asthma. *J Allergy Clin Immunol* **108** (Suppl 5): S147–S334.

British Thoracic Society/Scottish Intercollegiate Guideline Network. (2003). British guideline on the management of asthma. *Thorax* **58** (Suppl 1): i1–i94.

Chapter 8

Asthma in special circumstances

Patrick S. Fitch and Graeme P. Currie

Key points

- During pregnancy, the clinical control of asthma improves in one-third, remains the same in one-third and deteriorates in one-third.
- The general principles of asthma management are the same in pregnant as in non-pregnant women.
- Drugs used in the management of acute and chronic asthma are generally safe for use in pregnancy.
- During an acute exacerbation of asthma in pregnancy, hypoxia and hypotension should be aggressively managed; early obstetric and intensive care advice should be obtained where necessary.
- Individuals with features of active asthma should avoid underwater diving.
- Most asthmatics can fly in commercial aircraft without risk of adverse event; some hypoxic patients with advanced disease may require supplemental in-flight oxygen.

8.1 Pregnancy

Asthma is one of the most common chronic conditions that affect women during pregnancy (4–12% of pregnancies). When asthma is poorly controlled, there are potentially serious consequences for both the mother and unborn child. For example, retrospective studies have indicated that uncontrolled asthma can be associated with adverse outcomes in pregnancy such as pre-term birth, low birth weight and pre-eclampsia. It is often quoted that the clinical control of asthma improves in about one-third of women during pregnancy, remains the same in one-third and deteriorates in one-third, although it is more likely to deteriorate in those with more severe disease. The reasons for this and the mechanisms involved remain to be elucidated.

However, a number of known factors that are likely to influence the course of asthma during pregnancy are known. For example:

- the maternal immune system is altered during pregnancy, so that the foetus (genetically different) does not under go immunological rejection
- the presence of a female foetus is associated with worsening of asthma control
- a perception commonly exists that medication during pregnancy harms the foetus (this may lead to reduced compliance with inhaled corticosteroids)
- poorly controlled or severe asthma is associated with greater frequency of exacerbations and poorer asthma control during pregnancy
- modified cell-mediated immunity during pregnancy may alter the maternal response to inflammation and susceptibility to infection
- cigarette smoking and obesity contribute to deteriorating asthma control during pregnancy

8.1.1 **Clinical features**

Clinicians should be aware that clinical features of asthma are similar in the pregnant and non-pregnant state. Ideally, pregnant women with asthma should be assessed every month. During a consultation, it is helpful to determine by subjective and objective means, the level of asthma control. Inadequate control may be indicated by the presence of daytime and nocturnal symptoms and increased frequency of reliever use. Some patients have a reduced perception of symptoms of significant airflow obstruction and in certain circumstances it is useful to monitor control by daily peak expiratory flow (PEF) recordings. A diurnal variation of greater than 20% is regarded as significant and suggests less well controlled asthma.

8.1.2 **Acute asthma**

Acute exacerbations of asthma are more likely to occur towards the end of the second trimester or third trimester, although they are less common during labour. The diagnosis of acute asthma will more likely be made in a patient with known disease, although it can present for the first time during pregnancy. Recent prospective studies have shown that where exacerbations are managed appropriately, there is no excess risk of pregnancy complications, which in turn emphasizes the importance of rapid assessment and adequate treatment.

In pregnant women admitted to hospital for suspected acute asthma, the diagnosis rests heavily on history and examination findings. It is important to remember that breathlessness in a pregnant woman with a history of asthma is not always due to heightened airway inflammation and bronchoconstriction. The differential diagnosis includes:

- pulmonary embolism
- pneumothorax
- pneumonia
- hyperventilation (whether due to anxiety or physiological response to pregnancy)
- amniotic fluid embolism
- peripartum cardiomyopathy
- pulmonary oedema

In some cases a chest radiograph is indicated to rule out other potential diagnoses such as pneumothorax or pneumonia. The dose of radiation involved in a single chest radiograph is small and where the potential risk of missing other diagnoses outweighs any risks to the foetus, expectant mothers should not be declined this investigation. Pregnant women admitted to medical wards for acute asthma should be referred promptly to the local obstetric service and those in the second or third trimester should have continuous foetal monitoring when asthma is severe or uncontrolled.

8.1.3 Management

The aim of treatment of chronic asthma during pregnancy is to produce a situation where the patient has minimal or no symptoms and does not require regular use of β_2-agonists to relieve symptoms. General measures involved in overall management include patient education, smoking cessation advice, avoidance of trigger factors where possible and relaxation techniques. During an acute exacerbation, an important aim is to avoid hypoxic or hypotensive episodes in the mother (which may potentially harm the foetus) with the use of high flow oxygen and intravenous fluids where necessary. It might also be necessary to place some patients in the left lateral position to reduce pressure on the vena cava from a gravid uterus. Exacerbations should generally be treated aggressively, and early contact be made with the intensive care unit and obstetrician where necessary. Clinicians and expectant mothers alike should be aware that drugs used in the management of acute and chronic asthma are generally safe for use in pregnancy, and the risks of poorly controlled asthma far outweigh any potential risk arising from most treatments.

8.1.4 Inhaled corticosteroids

Extensive experience with and surveillance of inhaled corticosteroids during pregnancy have indicated their safety. Inhaled corticosteroids are not generally absorbed into the body in any significant quantities, while the enzyme 11β-hydroxysteroid dehydrogenase in the placenta metabolizes a variety of corticosteroids, including betamethasone, beclometasone, dexamethasone and prednisolone. Fluticasone and budesonide are not metabolized by this enzyme, but studies have not shown any adverse effects on the foetus due to these inhaled corticosteroids. Women with asthma using inhaled corticosteroids should therefore be encouraged to continue taking these drugs throughout pregnancy.

8.1.5 Oral corticosteroids

Oral corticosteroids have been implicated in causing a slight increase in the rate of cleft palate in children born to mothers who received them in the first trimester. However, it is difficult to tease out in studies whether it was the use of oral corticosteroids or the severity of asthma that caused the increased incidence of the abnormality. Moreover, in one study there were reasons other than asthma for taking corticosteroids and the duration of oral corticosteroid use was longer than is generally used for acute asthma. Whatever the cause of the association, the absolute increase in risk of cleft palate is small (0.1% to 0.3%). It is also possible that oral corticosteroid use in pregnancy can result in lower birth weight children. In general, it seems sensible to treat asthma exacerbations with short courses of prednisolone as for non-pregnant patients, as the risks of uncontrolled exacerbations are likely to be greater than any harm to the foetus.

8.1.6 β₂-agonists

Large studies have indicated that β_2-agonists are generally safe during pregnancy and breastfeeding. However, long-acting β_2-agonists (salmeterol, formoterol) should only be used in combination with an inhaled corticosteroid (i.e. not as monotherapy) where the latter alone has failed to control symptoms.

8.1.7 Leukotriene receptor antagonists

Animal data have indicated that leukotriene receptor antagonists are not likely to be teratogenic, although data in human pregnancies have so far been limited to small studies. However, the available literature in humans suggests that these drugs do not confer adverse effects either on the foetus or on the course of pregnancy. At present, the recommendation is that leukotriene receptor antagonists should not be initiated during pregnancy, but may be continued if a patient has severe asthma not adequately controlled on inhaled corticosteroids and long-acting β_2-agonists.

8.1.8 Other drugs

Theophylline, aminophylline and intravenous magnesium are not contraindicated in pregnancy.

8.2 Underwater diving

British Thoracic Society guidelines on respiratory aspects of fitness for diving indicate that patients with asthma should be advised *not* to dive if they have wheeze precipitated by exercise, cold or emotion. However, individuals with asthma may be permitted to dive–with or without regular anti-inflammatory treatment–if they have:

- no symptoms of active asthma
- normal spirometry
- a negative exercise test (regarded as a less than 15% fall in forced expiratory volume in 1 second (FEV_1) following exercise)

The guidelines further suggest that they should also monitor their asthma with twice daily PEF recordings, and avoid diving if they have:

- active asthma (defined as symptoms requiring relief medication in 48 hours preceding a dive)
- reduced PEF (>10% fall from best values)
- increased PEF variability (>20% diurnal variability)

8.3 Flying

Most individuals with asthma can safely fly and are not expected to experience any adverse effects from doing so. It is important that patients take reliever inhalers onto the flight with hand luggage, while nebulizers may be used at the discretion of the particular airline. Some patients with asthma who experience frequent exacerbations may find it useful to take a short course of prednisolone for use in an emergency when travelling abroad.

A small proportion of individuals with chronic asthma, especially elderly patients with advanced disease and a previous history of smoking, may be hypoxic while breathing room air (21% oxygen). Even in healthy subjects, the partial pressure of oxygen falls at altitude, which might compound any respiratory difficulties encountered with a hypoxaemic individual during a flight. Commercial aircraft are pressurized to a cabin pressure of 2438 m (8000 feet), at which the partial pressure in arterial blood falls to the equivalent of breathing approximately 15% oxygen at sea level. In patients who have an adequate partial oxygen pressure at sea level, oxygenation may fall below desirable levels when cabin altitude is simulated. This desaturation is exacerbated by minimal exercise.

In potentially hypoxic patients, the oxygen saturation on air using a pulse oximeter should be measured before flights are booked. This in turn will help determine whether in-flight oxygen is required or not (Table 8.1). All individuals who require in-flight oxygen should inform the relevant airline when booking and be aware that some airlines charge for this service. Moreover, any need for oxygen on the ground and while changing flights must also be considered.

Table 8.1 Advice regarding necessity (or otherwise) of in-flight oxygen in commercial aircraft

Oxygen saturation on air	Recommendation
>95%	Oxygen not required
92–95% (without risk factor*)	Oxygen not required
92–95% (with risk factor*)	Hypoxic challenge test†
<92%	In-flight oxygen required (2 or 4 L/min)
Already receiving long-term oxygen therapy	Increase flow rate

* Risk factor: FEV_1 <50% predicted, lung cancer, respiratory muscle weakness and other restrictive ventilatory disorders, within 6 weeks of hospital discharge.

† This involves subjects breathing 15% oxygen at sea level to mimic the environment with reduced inspiratory oxygen pressure to which they would be exposed during a typical commercial flight. Those with pO_2 >7.4 kPa post hypoxic challenge do not require in-flight oxygen, those with pO_2 <6.6 kPa require in-flight oxygen, and those with pO_2 6.6–7.4 kPa are considered borderline.

Further reading

(2002). Managing passengers with respiratory disease planning air travel: British Thoracic Society recommendations. *Thorax* **57**: 289–304.

Blais L, Beauchesne MF, Rey E, Malo JL, Forget A. (2007). Use of inhaled corticosteroids during the first trimester of pregnancy and the risk of congenital malformations among women with asthma. *Thorax* **62**: 320–8.

Godden D, Currie GP, Denison D, *et al.* (2003). The British Thoracic Society guidelines on respiratory aspects of fitness for diving. *Thorax* **58**: 3–13.

Murphy VE, Clifton VL, Gibson PG. (2006). Asthma exacerbations during pregnancy: incidence and association with adverse pregnancy outcomes. *Thorax* **61**: 169–76.

Rey E, Boulet L. (2007). Asthma in pregnancy. *Br Med J* **334**: 582–5.

Chapter 9

Difficult asthma

Claire A. Butler and Liam G. Heaney

Key points

- Patients with 'difficult asthma' often have other factors causing them to respond poorly to conventional treatment; this term should not be confused with 'therapy-resistant asthma' or 'refractory asthma'.
- A number of key questions should be addressed when faced with a patient who appears to be responding poorly to therapy:
  - does the patient have asthma?
  - are they taking prescribed treatment?
  - are there additional aggravating factors?
- True therapy-resistant asthma occurs when the patient has persisting symptoms due to asthma and the three key questions above have been addressed.

9.1 Introduction

Most patients with asthma respond to standard doses of inhaled corticosteroids with or without additional therapies such as long-acting β_2-agonists, theophyllines or leukotriene receptor antagonists. For example, the Gaining Optimal Asthma Control (GOAL) study indicated that the majority of patients (around 80%) would have well controlled asthma when treated with a combination of inhaled corticosteroid and long-acting β_2-agonist. Effective treatment, along with asthma action plans, should mean that the substantial majority of patients can expect minimal breakthrough symptoms on standard doses of inhaled regimes. However, a small group of patients can present with persisting symptoms despite effective therapy, and are often referred to as having 'difficult to control asthma'.

9.2 Difficult asthma

A pragmatic definition of difficult asthma is persistent respiratory symptoms, despite treatment with a long-acting β_2-agonist and inhaled corticosteroids (≥800 micrograms beclometasone equivalent) and at least one course of rescue corticosteroids in the preceding 12 months. This equates with subjects who remain symptomatic at step 4 or those requiring treatment at step 5 of the British Thoracic Society/Scottish Intercollegiate Guidelines Network (BTS/SIGN) guidelines on the management of asthma. It is estimated that between 5% and 10% of adult patients fulfill this definition, although the prevalence has not been precisely determined.

It is important to differentiate the term 'difficult asthma' from 'therapy-resistant asthma' or 'refractory asthma'. The latter two terms encompass patients who are relatively treatment resistant and generally require high doses of inhaled corticosteroids to achieve symptom control, while patients with difficult asthma often have many different factors that cause them to respond poorly to treatment. It is important to adopt a systematic approach to the assessment and management of this group of patients, and a number of key questions should be asked before committing individuals to further high dose treatment.

9.2.1 Does the patient have asthma?

When faced with a difficult asthmatic who is not responding to conventional therapy, it is important to first confirm the diagnosis by reviewing the history and objective corroborative measures of asthma, such as reversible airflow obstruction. If satisfied that the patient definitely has asthma, it is then important to identify other concomitant conditions that may result in asthma-like symptoms, which are often inappropriately treated as asthma. Alternative diagnoses are commonly identified after systematic evaluation and have amounted to 19% (Brompton study) and 34% (Belfast study) in two published case series of difficult asthmatics (Table 9.1). When these conditions are correctly identified and managed, this should generally lead to an improvement in symptom control, without escalating therapy. It is important to re-emphasise that in many cases, these alternative conditions and asthma co-exist. For example, around one-third of patients with vocal cord dysfunction are reported to also have asthma.

Other less common diagnoses found in the two cohorts included chronic bronchitis, immunoglobulin A (IgA) deficiency, cystic fibrosis, obliterative bronchiolitis, cardiomyopathy, pulmonary hypertension, hypereosinophilia, extrinsic allergic alveolitis, respiratory muscle incoordination and obstructive sleep apnoea.

Thus, many other conditions can cause asthma-like symptoms, and not surprisingly are associated with a poor response to asthma therapy. Identification and management of these should improve symptoms and allow a reduction of asthma medication. Asthma treatment is not without side effects, and this is particularly the case for recurrent systemic corticosteroid exposure.

Table 9.1 Common alternative/concomitant diagnoses in difficult asthma		
Alternative condition	Diagnosis	Management
Bronchiectasis	Steroid-unresponsive productive cough Recurrent bacterial infection with sputum purulence Typical HRCT findings	Training in mucus clearance techniques Antibiotic treatment of infections Maintenance macrolide therapy
Dysfunctional breathlessness/ hyperventilation syndrome	Atypical symptoms and exertional breathlessness out of keeping with lung function	Explanation Graded exercise programme
Chronic obstructive pulmonary disease (COPD)	Fixed airflow obstruction Exertional dyspnoea unresponsive to increasing medication	Bronchodilators Pulmonary rehabilitation
Vocal cord dysfunction	Inspiratory stridor when symptomatic (due to paradoxical inspiratory vocal cord adduction) Variable inspiratory and expiratory flow volume loops	Speech and language therapy Treatment of psychological co-morbidity

9.2.2 Is the patient taking their treatment?

Poor adherence is present throughout the spectrum of asthma severity and is an important reason for an apparent poor response to treatment. Both patient and physician reporting are recognized to be consistently unreliable. Direct measurements such as plasma theophylline levels or plasma prednisolone and cortisol measurements are useful in some patients. Assessment of adherence to inhaled therapy is difficult, although surrogate measures such as prescription filling of maintenance inhalers can be useful. A recent study of non-adherence in a difficult asthmatic population of 182 patients found that 34% were collecting less than 50% of their prescribed inhaled medication. Moreover, approximately 50% of patients on maintenance oral corticosteroid were found to be non-adherent when plasma prednisolone and cortisol levels were assessed in two case series of difficult asthmatics. Despite ongoing asthma symptoms, many patients choose not to take their treatment as prescribed and the issues underlying non-adherence must be explored. Poor adherence may result from a number of factors including:

- fear of adverse effects
- lack of immediate effect following inhaled corticosteroids
- poor education
- resentment by adolescents about the need for therapy
- economic restriction on access to health care
- demographic factors such as sex and ethnicity
- secondary gain from ongoing symptoms

It can be difficult to question patients regarding poor adherence as this can lead to breakdown of the physician–patient relationship, and therefore needs to be addressed in an empathetic and non-confrontational manner. The key issue is identifying the particular reason for non-adherence in an individual. Adequate education can allay any fears that a patient may have regarding treatment, especially the potential adverse effects of corticosteroids. Respiratory nurse specialists may have an important role to play in this area.

9.2.3 Are there additional aggravating factors?

It is important to identify other factors that may be driving asthma symptoms, and these include:

- intrinsic factors:
  - psychological factors
  - upper airways disease
  - gastro-oesophegal reflux
  - systemic disease (thyrotoxicosis, Churg–Strauss syndrome, carcinoid syndrome)
- extrinsic factors:
  - drugs
  - inhaled allergen exposure
  - occupational factors

9.2.4 Intrinsic factors

There is a much debated link between asthma control and psychological stress. It is likely that difficult to control asthma results in considerable psychological stress for patients, especially if there has been a history of life-threatening exacerbations. However, it is also likely that psychological factors themselves can worsen asthma control. Indeed, psychosocial morbidity has been associated with asthma death and near fatal asthma. In the Belfast study, psychiatric morbidity was common when formally assessed by a medical liaison psychiatrist, with 32 of 65 (49%) sequential patients having an International Classification of Disease-10 (ICD10) psychiatric diagnosis, most commonly depression. The Hospital Anxiety and Depression Scale (HADS) had a good negative predictive value for depression. Interestingly, having a psychiatric diagnosis with targeted management was not associated with a better asthma outcome. In the Brompton cohort, 33 of 56 (58%) subjects had a psychiatric component to their asthma and in 10 this was identified as 'major' (defined as 30% of symptomatic episodes related to feeling tense or subjects saying this was 'why I get breathless'). However, it remains unclear if a 'cause' or 'effect' relationship exists between this observed psychological morbidity and difficult asthma, and whether treatment of coexistent psychiatric morbidity improves asthma outcome. In addition, while acute stress and depression are often identified by patients as triggers, the impact of these psychological factors on asthma control may manifest as poor adherence with prescribed therapy, rather than as a direct effect on asthma severity.

Many patients with asthma have coexistent allergic rhinitis or sinus disease. A pragmatic approach is to give a trial of nasal corticosteroid spray/antihistamine for symptomatic nasal disease and consider specialist review if there is a failure of therapy, to determine if there is a structural component that would be amenable to surgical intervention. In some patients, managing their nasal disease can have a significant benefit on overall symptom control.

Although the incidence of gastro-oesophageal reflux disease (GORD) is higher in asthmatic patients than the general population, there is no convincing evidence to support improved asthma control with antireflux strategies. Continuous oral prednisolone has been shown to increase GORD, and this may exacerbate the problem in difficult asthmatics having frequent exposure to this medication. A pragmatic approach is to give a trial of standard therapy (proton pump inhibition such as omeprazole or lansoprazole) if symptomatic reflux is present, but the evidence for an aggressive investigative strategy for 'silent reflux' with pH profiling is lacking.

Rare systemic diseases such as thyrotoxicosis, carcinoid syndrome and Churg–Strauss syndrome may cause poor asthma control and should be considered as part of a detailed evaluation.

9.2.5 Extrinsic factors

A number of drugs may worsen asthma control, including β-blockers (including topical eye drops), non-steroidal anti-inflammatory drugs and aspirin. These are commonly avoided by asthmatic patients and alternative analgesics and antihypertensive agents should be used. Occupational factors may play a part in poor disease control, although many patients with difficult asthma have stopped work because of their symptoms. Exposure to inhaled allergens (house dust mite, fungal allergens, cat allergens, etc.) can be an important driving factor in persistent asthma symptoms, and changes in living conditions or acquisition of a new pet should be identified with a thorough history. Although there is a relative lack of evidence supporting avoidance of house dust mite and other ubiquitous allergens, removal of pets, if sensitized, seems appropriate (although this advice is frequently ignored).

9.3 **True therapy-resistant asthma**

Therapy-resistant asthma occurs when persistent symptoms exist despite high dose inhaled corticosteroids (2000 micrograms/day of beclometasone or equivalent) plus long-acting β_2-agonists with either maintenance systemic corticosteroids or at least two rescue courses of corticosteroids over 12 months and despite trials of other add-on therapy. This term assumes that the patient has been systematically evaluated and the issues, as mentioned above, have been addressed. In general, following systematic evaluation and a detailed analysis of all the issues, one-third to one-half of patients referred with difficult asthma will not have therapy-resistant disease.

Complete corticosteroid resistance is uncommon, and patients with therapy resistance are 'relatively' corticosteroid resistant and tend to respond to higher doses of treatment, usually given systemically. In subjects requiring unacceptable doses of systemic corticosteroids, a trial of an immunosuppressive agent is often given, principally as a corticosteroid sparing medication. The most commonly used immunosuppressive agents for refractory asthma are ciclosporin and methotrexate, although they have a significant adverse effect profile and limited efficacy.

It is important to assess all difficult asthmatic patients for the presence of osteoporosis with dual energy X-ray absorptiometry (DEXA) scanning as many patients will have had considerable systemic corticosteroid exposure. Patients should be prescribed calcium and vitamin D supplements or a bisphosphonate, in accordance with appropriate management guidelines, particularly for patients requiring frequent 'bursts' of (or maintenance) systemic corticosteroids.

Further research into alternative asthma therapy for these patients is important due to the significant adverse effects of long-term oral prednisolone, which have been outlined Chapter 4. In order to identify the mechanisms that underpin therapy-resistant asthma it is important to ensure that patients included in both mechanistic and therapeutic research programmes are well characterized. This is most likely to be achieved through the use of systematic evaluation protocols at specialist centres. When faced with a patient with seemingly difficult asthma it is important to adopt a systematic approach as summarized in Figure 9.1.

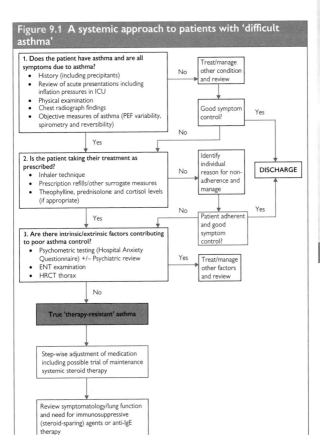

Figure 9.1 A systemic approach to patients with 'difficult asthma'

9.4 Conclusion

Difficult asthma requires a systematic approach to identify factors contributing to persisting symptoms, before a patient is labelled as having refractory asthma. Appropriate management of these factors should allow many patients to return to standard doses of inhaled medication or even complete withdrawal of treatment if they do not have asthma. Patients with true therapy-resistant asthma usually require ongoing high dose treatment and careful clinical follow-up.

Further reading

Barnes PJ, Woolcock AJ. (1998). Difficult asthma. *Eur Respir J* **12**: 1209–18.

Bateman ED, Boushey HA, Bousquet J, Busse WW, Clark TJ, Pauwels RA, Pedersen SE; GOAL Investigators Group. (2004). Can guideline-defined asthma control be achieved? The Gaining Optimal Asthma Control Study. *Am J Respir Crit Care Med* **170**: 836–44.

Heaney LG, Conway E, Kelly C, Johnston BT, English C, Stevenson M, Gamble J. (2003). Predictors of therapy resistant asthma: outcome of a systematic evaluation protocol. *Thorax* **58**: 561–6.

Robinson DS, Campbell DA, Durham SR, Pfeffer J, Barnes PJ, Chung KF. (2003). Systematic assessment of difficult-to-treat asthma. *Eur Respir J* **22**: 478–83.

Chapter 10

New treatments and the future

Graeme P. Currie

Key points

- Once-daily inhaled corticosteroids with fewer adverse effects due to 'on site' lung activation provide an increasingly attractive therapeutic option.
- Ultra long-acting β_2-agonists are in varying stages of development and confer a quick onset and prolonged period of bronchodilatation.
- Certain inhaled corticosteroid plus long-acting β_2-agonist preparations (Symbicort®) may be used both for relief and prevention of symptoms.
- Anti-immunoglobulin E is a novel approach to the treatment of asthma. It is of some use in more severe allergic asthma, although long-term studies are needed to evaluate long-term effects, overall cost reduction and patient acceptability.
- Selective phosphodiesterase inhibitors confer weak anti-inflammatory and bronchodilator properties without some of the adverse effects experienced with non-selective phosphodiesterase inhibitors.
- Bronchial thermoplasty is a novel treatment for asthma whereby controlled thermal energy is delivered to the airway wall during bronchoscopy.
- Titrating asthma treatment based on non-invasive measures of underlying inflammation (such as exhaled nitric oxygen and airway eosinophils) has been shown to be more effective than altering treatment according to conventional parameters alone.

10.1 **Drugs**

10.1.1 **Novel inhaled corticosteroids**

Although inhaled corticosteroids are a fundamental component in the management of asthma, compliance is frequently poor in many individuals, in part due to concerns regarding long-term systemic and local adverse effects. Ciclesonide is a novel lipophilic inhaled corticosteroid that has recently become licensed in the UK for once-daily use in asthma. It represents an exciting development as it becomes activated in the lung by esterase cleavage, in turn obviating problems of untoward extra-pulmonary adverse effects. The unique pharmacological properties of ciclesonide, fewer local adverse effects and limited effect upon the hypothalamic–pituitary–adrenal axis due to 'on site' lung activation (in addition to its once-daily dosing regime), makes it particularly attractive in encouraging compliance without the concerns of local and systemic complications.

10.1.2 **Ultra long-acting β_2-agonists**

Since long-acting β_2-agonists play a pivotal and widespread role in the management of moderate to severe asthma, any attempt to facilitate patient compliance and preference with once-daily dosing can be seen to be an advantageous step forward. Several different ultra long-acing β_2-agonists such as arfomoterol, carmoterol and indacaterol are in varying degrees of clinical development. Moreover, it is conceivable that with ultra long-acing β_2-agonists such as indacaterol, which also relaxes airway smooth muscle within 5 minutes of dosing, patients will be able to perceive a relatively quick onset of bronchodilatation. This in turn may encourage compliance *per se* in addition to improved compliance associated longer term benefits, such as fewer exacerbations and better quality of life. Perhaps, in the future, fixed dose combinations of long-acting inhaled corticosteroids and ultra long-acting β_2-agonists may permit once-daily dosing regimes in patients requiring both classes of drug.

10.1.3 **Combination inhalers for the relief and prevention of symptoms**

Due to the relatively quick onset of action of long-acting β_2-agonists, fixed combination inhalers have been evaluated for use on both a once-daily and 'as required' fashion in some clinical trials. For example, in a double blind, randomized, parallel-group study involving 2760 asthmatics, the combination of budesonide plus formoterol in a single inhaler used regularly and on an 'as required' basis, prolonged the time to first severe exacerbation (P <0.001), resulting in a 45–47% lower exacerbation risk versus budesonide plus formoterol with an 'as required' short-acting β_2-agonist. Moreover, in the same study, the combination inhaler when used on a regular basis in addition to 'as required' use, was not associated with an excessive burden of inhaled corticosteroid. In the future it is therefore possible that in patients who need treatment at step 3 of the pharmacological escalator, a single fixed dose inhaler may facilitate both relief and prevention of symptoms. In the UK, certain formulations of budesonide plus formoterol (Symbicort®) have been licensed to be used in this manner, although it is unlikely that the combination of salmeterol plus fluticasone (Seretide®) will ever be used in this way as adverse effects occur with cumulative doses of salmeterol, which also has a slower onset of action (compared to formoterol).

10.1.4 Leukotriene receptor antagonists

Studies comparing the effects of either a leukotriene receptor antagonist or long-acting β_2-agonist on lung function alone, tend to favour the latter drug since it more potently relaxes bronchial smooth muscle. However, several trials have performed head-to-head comparisons of either drug as therapeutic additions to inhaled corticosteroids using exacerbation frequency as the primary endpoint. Most studies that have made direct comparisons of leukotriene receptor antagonists versus long-acting β_2-agonists, demonstrate that the addition of either drug to an inhaled corticosteroid is generally as effective as the other in reducing exacerbations. Moreover, the addition of a long-acting β_2-agonist is consistently superior to a leukotriene receptor antagonist in improving lung function, while the latter treatment confers anti-inflammatory activity and attenuates airway hyperresponsiveness to a greater extent. Whether these observations will lead to future guidelines in asthma management acknowledging that the addition of a leukotriene receptor antagonist at step 3 may be as effective as adding a long-acting β_2-agonist in reducing exacerbations remains to be seen.

10.1.5 New phosphodiesterase inhibitors

Theophylline is a non-selective phosphodiesterase inhibitor and indiscriminately inhibits izoenzymes in many cell types and organs of the body. It can therefore be reasoned that a derivative of theophylline (with more selective phosphodiesterase isoenzyme inhibition), could theoretically confer greater benefits in the overall treatment of asthma.

The isoenzyme phosphodiesterase-4 is expressed in many pro-inflammatory cells found in the airway including neutrophils, macrophages, eosinophils, mast cells and lymphocytes. Phosphodiesterase-4 inhibitors have been developed and exhibit a range of immunomodulatory effects such as reduced cytokine and chemokine release, reduced microvascular leakage, an inhibitory effect upon inflammatory cells, attenuation of adhesion molecule expression, impaired reactive oxygen species production and inhibition of cellular proliferation.

Roflumilast (Figure 10.1) is a second generation phosphodiesterase-4 inhibitor and is the most clinically advanced drug of this class undergoing evaluation for use in asthma. However, further research is required to establish whether phosphodiesterase-4 inhibitors do have a definite place in the stepwise management of asthma and exhibit a superior therapeutic ratio compared to non-selective phosphodiesterase inhibition. Not only are studies required to determine whether they might have a role in some mild asthmatics as monotherapy, but it is also important to determine whether they could be of benefit as add-on therapy to existing treatments.

10.1.6 **Anti-immunoglobulin E**

Many individuals with asthma are atopic, with the consequence that aeroallergens interact with immunoglobulin E (IgE) and cause the release of inflammatory mediators. Humanized recombinant mono-clonal anti-IgE antibodies have been developed for the treatment of IgE-mediated disease processes. These drugs attenuate the activity of IgE by linking to the constant region of the IgE molecule, which prevents circulating IgE from interacting with receptors on a variety of inflammatory cells (Figure 10.2).

Figure 10.1 The chemical structure of roflumilast

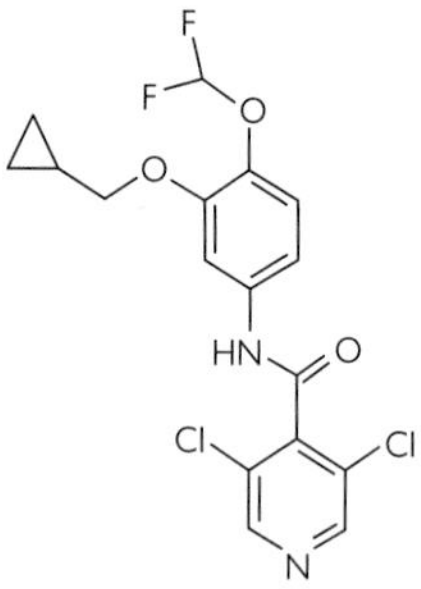

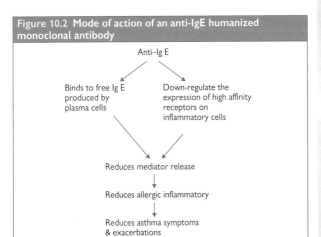

Figure 10.2 Mode of action of an anti-IgE humanized monoclonal antibody

Anti–Ig E

Binds to free Ig E produced by plasma cells

Down-regulate the expression of high affinity receptors on inflammatory cells

Reduces mediator release

Reduces allergic inflammatory

Reduces asthma symptoms & exacerbations

Omalizumab is the most clinically advanced recombinant monoclonal antibody and has been shown to be useful in patients with allergic inflammatory disorders. In several trials in the asthmatic population, it has been shown to reduce symptoms, reduce the number of exacerbations, improve quality of life, and facilitate a reduction in inhaled corticosteroid dose. It has also been shown to have beneficial effects in patients with asthma and concomitant allergic rhinitis. In the Innovate study, the addition of omalizumab to inhaled corticosteroids plus long-acting β_2-agonists in severe asthmatics conferred clinically significant reductions in exacerbations and improvements in quality of life and lung function. Further studies are required to evaluate the 'real life' effectiveness and patient acceptability of omalizumab and other future anti-IgE molecules, especially given the fact that it is administered by subcutaneous injection at regular intervals.

10.1.7 Anti-tumour necrosis factor monoclonal antibodies

Interest has grown regarding the potential role of tumour necrosis factor alpha (TNFα) in chronic inflammatory conditions such as rheumatoid arthritis and inflammatory bowel disease. Given the promising effects of monoclonal antibodies against TNFα in these conditions, several studies have also evaluated their effects in refractory asthma. Initial data have shown some promise with drugs such as etanercept and infliximab in improving symptoms and lung function, and reducing airway hyperresponsiveness. Further long-term, larger studies are required to more fully evaluate their putative benefits and adverse effect profiles.

10.2 **Other advances**

10.2.1 **Pharmacological treatment of the unified airway**

Since the upper and lower airways share anatomical continuity, epithelial lining and release similar inflammatory mediators, it has been suggested that asthma and allergic rhinitis represent a continuation of the same inflammatory disease process. Moreover, successful treatment of allergic rhinitis can confer benefits in overall asthma control. In this respect, anti-inflammatory treatment (usually with nasal cortico-steroids) should usually be directed towards the upper airway in persistent asthmatics with features of symptomatic allergic rhinitis. Increasingly, leukotriene receptor antagonists have been shown to be useful in individuals with both allergic rhinitis and concomitant asthma. For example, in a multicentre trial, the efficacy of leukotriene receptor antagonists in individuals ($n = 831$) with both symptomatic allergic rhinitis and active asthma was evaluated. Subjects were randomized to receive daily montelukast 10 mg ($n = 415$) or placebo ($n = 416$) in a 2-week, double-blind treatment period. Montelukast significantly ($P = 0.001$) reduced rhinitis symptom scores compared to placebo, with improvements also being observed in nasal and eye symptoms. Moreover, montelukast provided benefit in overall asthma control and reduced the requirement for reliever use. Whether in the future a therapeutic trial of leukotriene receptor antagonist becomes standard practice in individuals symptomatic of both upper and lower airways inflammation remains to be seen.

10.2.2 **Non-invasive methods of titrating asthma treatment**

Partly due to the heterogeneity of asthma, one of the main problems in its management is difficulty in determining when inflammation has been adequately suppressed and concomitant non-steroidal second line controller therapy should be commenced or the inhaled corti-costeroid dose increased or decreased. In other words, the decision when to start further second line therapy or to titrate the inhaled corticosteroid dose is often fairly arbitrary. In an ideal world, clinicians would have access to a non-invasive simple test that would assist them in this respect. Unfortunately, there is no widely accepted and straightforward method of identifying airway inflammation, and the assessment of surrogate inflammatory biomarkers at present tends to be preserved for research purposes and specialized centres. However, non-invasive tools by which to measure the extent of underlying inflammation and to titrate anti-inflammatory treatment accordingly — for example exhaled nitric oxide, sputum eosinophils and airway hyperresponsiveness — have been studied with some success. Perhaps, in the future, measuring a surrogate inflammatory biomarker such as exhaled nitric oxide may become the norm before deciding to alter the inhaled corticosteroid dose or add in a further second line agent (Table 10.1).

10.2.3 Pharmacogenetics

Some patients appear to respond preferentially to different types of asthma controller therapy. This in turn has lead to interest relating to pharmacogenetic determinants that may influence the response to treatment in asthma. Polymorphisms of the β_2-adrenoceptor and leukotriene C_4 synthase (a crucial enzyme involved in the biosynthesis of cysteinyl leukotrienes) have been identified that may influence the individual response to treatment. In the future, clinical trials could be designed that specifically evaluate any preferential response according to the presence or absence of various polymorphisms. It is therefore conceivable that treatment could be tailored depending on the specific genotype of the patient.

> **Box 10.1 Characteristic features of the ideal surrogate inflammatory biomarker by which to monitor the response to treatment and subsequently titrate therapy**
>
> Raised only in asthma
> Raised only when endobronchial inflammation is present
> Portable
> Inexpensive
> Easy to measure in primary and secondary care settings
> Acceptable to patients
> Linear reduction on the institution of anti-inflammatory therapy with a demonstrable clear-cut dose–response effect
> Demonstrated to provide better clinical control when used along with conventional measures than with the latter alone

10.2.4 Bronchial thermoplasty

An increase in airway smooth muscle mass is often found in asthmatics, and is considered to be an important factor in those with severe or fatal asthma. Bronchial thermoplasty is a novel treatment still undergoing evaluation, where controlled thermal energy is delivered to the airway wall during several bronchoscopy procedures. This in turn results in a prolonged reduction of airway smooth muscle mass. In individuals with moderate to severe asthma, thermoplasty has been shown to confer some benefit in reducing symptoms, reliever use and exacerbations and in improving quality of life and lung function. Further large, long-term studies are required to fully evaluate this new procedure and determine which patients may benefit most.

Further reading

Berry MA, Hargadon B, Shelley M, et al. (2006). Evidence of a role of tumor necrosis factor alpha in refractory asthma. *N Engl J Med* **354**: 697–708.

Currie GP. (2006). Effects of asthma treatment: the present and future. *Expert Rev Clin Immunol* **2**: 547–60.

Currie GP, Lee DK, Srivastava P. (2005). Long-acting bronchodilator or leukotriene modifier as add-on therapy to inhaled corticosteroids in persistent asthma? *Chest* **128**: 2954–62.

Holgate S, Casale T, Wenzel S, Bousquet J, Deniz Y, Reisner C. (2005). The anti-inflammatory effects of omalizumab confirm the central role of IgE in allergic inflammation. *J Allergy Clin Immunol* **115**: 459–65.

Humbert M, Beasley R, Ayres J, et al. (2005). Benefits of omalizumab as add-on therapy in patients with severe persistent asthma who are inadequately controlled despite best available therapy (GINA 2002 step 4 treatment): INNOVATE. *Allergy* **60**: 309–16.

Lima JJ, Zhang S, Grant A, et al. (2006). Influence of leukotriene pathway polymorphisms on response to montelukast in asthma. *Am J Respir Crit Care Med* **173**: 379–85.

O'Byrne PM, Bisgaard H, Godard PP, et al. (2005). Budesonide/formoterol combination therapy as both maintenance and reliever medication in asthma. *Am J Respir Crit Care Med* **171**: 129–36.

Philip G, Nayak AS, Berger WE, et al. (2004). The effect of montelukast on rhinitis symptoms in patients with asthma and seasonal allergic rhinitis. *Curr Med Res Opin* **20**: 1549–58.

Smith AD, Cowan JO, Brassett KP, Herbison GP, Taylor DR. (2005). Use of exhaled nitric oxide measurements to guide treatment in chronic asthma. *N Engl J Med* **352**: 2163–73.

Index

A

Accolate® 38
Accuhaler™ 43
action plans 24–5, 81
  allergen avoidance 26
  altering therapy 25
  complementary techniques 27
  dietary intervention 27
  smoking cessation 27–30
  what to do and how long to do it 25–6
acupuncture 27
acute cardiovascular disease 28
acute exacerbations
  admission to hospital 52
  aetiology 48
  clinical features 49–50
  discharge planning 56
  epidemiology 47
  investigations 50–1
  management 52–6
  pathogenesis 48–9
  pregnancy 52, 76–7, 78
  prevention 56
adherence to treatment 83–4
  new treatments 90
aetiology, acute exacerbations 48
age differences 2–3
airway hyperresponsiveness 95
airways, remodelling of 8, 9
allergens
  avoidance 26
  exacerbations of asthma 48
  prevalence of asthma 10
allergic asthma 13
allergic bronchopulmonary aspergillosis 21
allergic rhinitis see rhinitis, allergic
altering asthma therapy 25
aminophylline 53, 54–5
  pregnancy 79
antibiotics, acute exacerbations 55
anti-immunoglobulin E drugs 92–4
anti-tumour necrosis factor monoclonal antibodies 94
arfomoterol 90

arterial blood gases in exacerbations 50, 51
aspirin
  difficult asthma 85
  exacerbations of asthma 48
  as provoking stimulus 13
aspirin-sensitive asthma 20
  leukotriene receptor antagonists 39
asthmagens, occupational 60, 61, 63
atopic disease 3
  see also rhinitis, allergic

B

bacterial causes of exacerbations 48
beclometasone 33, 34, 35
  difficult asthma 81
  pregnancy 78
behavioural support, smoking cessation 27–8
β₂-agonists
  intravenous 53
  long-acting see long-acting β₂-agonists
  pregnancy 78
  reactive airways dysfunction syndrome 64
  short-acting see short-acting β₂-agonists
  ultra long-acting 90
betamethasone 78
biomarkers 18, 19, 95
British Thoracic Society (BTS) 69, 79, 82
brittle asthma 20
bronchial challenge testing 16–18
bronchial hyperresponsiveness/hyperreactivity 8
bronchiectasis 83
budesonide 33
  combination inhalers 36, 90–1
  pregnancy 78
bupropion 29–30
Buteyko technique 27

C

carbamazepine 40
carcinoid syndrome 85

cardiovascular disease, acute 28
carmoterol 90
cats 26, 85
chest radiographs
  diagnostic 18
  exacerbations 50, 51
  pregnancy 77
children
  acute exacerbations 47
  leukotriene receptor antagonists 38
chlorine gas 64
chronic obstructive pulmonary disease (COPD)
  bronchial challenge testing 16
  differential diagnosis 12
  difficult asthma 83
  spirometry 16
Churg–Strauss syndrome 20
  difficult asthma 85
  leukotriene receptor antagonists 39
ciclesonide 90
ciprofloxacin 40
clarithromycin 40
classical occupational asthma 59–60
  causes 60
  clinical features 61
  diagnosis 61–3
  legal issues 65
  management 63
  pathogenesis 61
  prognosis 64
cleft palate 78
clinical features 11, 13
  acute exacerbations 49–50
  differential diagnosis 11–13
  occupational asthma, classical 61
  in pregnancy 76
  subtypes of asthma 19, 20
  syndromes associated with asthma 18–19, 20–1
combination inhalers 36, 90–1
compensation, occupational asthma 65
complementary techniques 27
compliance with treatment 83–4
  new treatments 90

Control of Substances
    Hazardous to Health
    (COSHH) regulations
    63
COPD see chronic
    obstructive pulmonary
    disease
corticosteroids
    difficult asthma 84, 85
    education 84
    inhaled see inhaled
        corticosteroids
    intravenous 54
    nasal 85, 94
    oral see oral
        corticosteroids
    resistance to 86
COSHH regulations 63
costs of asthma 3, 4–5
    occupational asthma 64
cough
    causes 19
    reactive airways
        dysfunction syndrome
        64
cough variant asthma 19
cyclophosphamide 20
ciclosporin 86

D

deaths attributable to
    asthma 4, 47
definition of asthma 1–2
depression 84, 85
dexamethasone 78
diagnosis 11
    bronchial challenge testing
        16–18
    differential 11–13, 77
    difficult asthma 82
    inflammatory biomarkers
        18
    objective measures
        13–15
    occupational asthma,
        classical 61–2
    other investigations 18
    pregnancy 77
    primary care 70
    signs 13
    spirometry 15–16
    subtypes of asthma
        19, 20
    syndromes associated with
        asthma 18–19, 20–1
diet
    action plans 27
    prevalence of asthma 10
differential diagnosis
    11–13
    pregnancy 77
difficult asthma 81–2, 87
    aggravating factors 84–5
    does patient have asthma?
        82–3

is patient taking their
    treatment? 83–4
discharge planning 56
diving, underwater 79
dogs 26
drug causes of
    exacerbations 48
dry powder inhalers (DPIs)
    43
dysfunctional breathlessness/
    hyperventilation
    syndrome 83

E

Easi-breathe™ inhalers 43
eczema, atopic 13
    prevalence 3, 4
education programmes 24
    adherence to treatment
        84
    pregnancy 77
emergency treatment 4
environmental pollutants
    48
eosinophilia, sputum 18, 19,
    95
eosinophilic bronchitis 19
eosinophils 6–7
epidemiology 2–5
    acute exacerbations 47
epilepsy 29
erythromycin 40
etanercept 94
exacerbations see acute
    exacerbations
exercise-induced asthma 39
exercise testing 15
exhaled nitric oxide 95

F

feathers 26
FEV_1
    bronchial challenge testing
        17
    occupational asthma,
        classical 62
    spirometry 15–16
FEV_1/FVC ratio 15–16
fluticasone 33
    combination inhalers
        36, 91
    pregnancy 78
flying 79–80
forced expiratory volume in
    1 second see FEV_1
forced vital capacity (FVC)
    15–16
formoterol 34
    combination inhalers
        36, 90–1
    pregnancy 78
full blood count 18
FVC 15–16

G

Gaining Optimal Asthma
    Control (GOAL) study
    81
gastro-oesophageal reflux
    disease (GORD) 85
    chronic cough 19
gender differences 2–3
general practitioners see
    primary care
genetic factors 9
    differential diagnosis 13
    pharmacogenetics 95
geographical differences 2
glutaraldehyde asthma 63
goals of asthma
    management 23
GOAL study 81
gross pathology 5–6

H

hay fever 3, 4
hepatic impairment 38
herbal preparations 27
histamine
    bronchial challenge testing
        16
    occupational asthma,
        classical 62
histopathology 5–6
history taking
    occupational asthma 61
    primary care 70
homeopathy 27
hospital admissions 4, 52
    discharge planning 56
    management 52–6
    pregnancy 76
Hospital Anxiety and
    Depression Scale
    (HADS) 84
house dust mite
    avoidance 26
    difficult asthma 85
    prevalence of asthma
        10
humanized recombinant
    monoclonal anti-IgE
    antibodies 92–4
hydrocortisone 53, 54
hygiene, and prevalence of
    asthma 10
hypoxia, and flying 79–80

I

immediate hypersensitivity
    reaction 8
immunization, influenza 69
immunoglobulin E (IgE)
    6, 7–8, 9
    anti-IgE drugs 92–4
    diagnosis of asthma 18

occupational asthma, classical 61
impact of asthma 3–5
occupational asthma 64
inactivity 10
indacaterol 90
inflammatory biomarkers 18, 19, 95
infliximab 94
influenza immunization 69
inhaled corticosteroids 33–4, 81
  acute exacerbations 52–4
  adverse effects 34
  difficult asthma 81
  long-acting β₂-agonists combined with 35, 36
  novel 90
  occupational asthma, classical 63
  pregnancy 76, 77–8
  primary care 68
  reactive airways dysfunction syndrome 64
  therapy-resistant asthma 82, 86
inhalers 31, 42–3
  for adults 43–4
  combination 36, 90–1
  difficult asthma 83
  flying 79
  and nebulizers 44–5
  spacers, use and maintenance of 44
interleukins 6
intravenous β₂-agonists 53
intravenous corticosteroids 54
invasive ventilatory support, acute exacerbations 55
investigations of acute exacerbations 50–1
ipratropium 53, 54
isocyanates 64
itraconazole 21

L

lansoprazole 85
late phase reaction 8
latex asthma 63
legal issues, occupational asthma 65
leukotriene receptor antagonists 37–9, 81, 91
  acute exacerbations 55
  adverse effects 39
  allergic rhinitis 94
  pregnancy 78
lithium 40
long-acting β₂-agonists 34–5, 81
  adverse effects 35–6
  difficult asthma 81

inhaled corticosteroids combined with 35, 36
  and leukotriene receptor antagonists 91
  occupational asthma, classical 63
  pregnancy 78
  therapy-resistant asthma 86
  ultra 90
lymphocytes 6, 7

M

magnesium 53, 54
  pregnancy 79
maternal cigarette smoking 27
methacholine
  bronchial challenge testing 16, 17, 18
  occupational asthma, classical 62–3
  reactive airways dysfunction syndrome 64
methotrexate 86
mineral supplementation 27
montelukast 37
  chemical structure 38
  prescribing and pharmacokinetic data 38
  rhinitis, allergic 94
mortality rate 4, 47

N

nasal corticosteroids 85, 94
nebulizers 44–5
  acute exacerbations 52
  flying 79
new treatments
  bronchial thermoplasty 96
  drugs 90–4
  non-invasive methods of titrating asthma treatment 94–5
  pharmacogenetics 95
  pharmacological treatment of unified airway 94
nicotine replacement therapy 28–30
nitric oxide, exhaled 95
non-adherence to treatment 83–4
  new treatment 90
non-invasive methods of titrating asthma treatment 94–5
non-invasive ventilation (NIV), acute exacerbations 55
non-pharmacological management 23
  action plans 24–30
  education programmes 24

O

OASYS 62
obesity
  action plans 27
  pregnancy 76
  prevalence of asthma 10
occupational asthma 59–60
  causes 60
  classical 60–4
  clinical features 61
  diagnosis 61–3
  difficult asthma 85
  legal issues 65
  management 63
  pathogenesis 61
  prognosis 64
  reactive airways dysfunction syndrome 64
  referral to secondary care 70
  work-aggravated asthma 64
omalizumab 93–4
omeprazole 85
oral corticosteroids 40
  acute exacerbations 54
  adverse effects 41–2
  difficult asthma 83
  pregnancy 78
osteoporosis 86
oxygen
  acute exacerbations 52, 53, 56, 77
  flying 79–80
  pregnancy 77
  primary care 68

P

pathogenesis
  of acute exacerbations 48–9
  occupational asthma, classical 61
pathology 5–6
pathophysiology 3
  eosinophils 6–7
  immunoglobulin E 7–8, 9
  lymphocytes 6, 7
  remodelling of airways 8
PC₂₀ see provocative dose/concentration
PD₂₀ see provocative dose/concentration
peak expiratory flow (PEF)
  action plans 25
  acute exacerbations 52
  education programmes 24
  occupational asthma, classical 61–2
  pregnancy 76
  reversibility 14–15
  underwater diving 79
  variability 14, 15

peak flow meters 14, 15
personalized action plans
  see action plans
pets 26, 85
pharmacogenetics 95
pharmacological
  management 31–2
  inhaled corticosteroids
    33–4
  inhalers see inhalers
  leukotriene receptor
    antagonists 37–9
  long-acting β₂-agonists
    34–6
  oral corticosteroids 40–2
  short-acting β₂-agonists
    33
  theophylline 39–40
phenytoin 40
phosphodiesterase inhibitors
  91–2, 93
pneumothorax 50, 51
pollutants 48
post-nasal drip syndrome
  19
pranlukast 37
prednisolone 40, 42
  acute exacerbations
    53, 54, 56
  difficult asthma 83, 85, 87
  flying 79
  gastro-oesophageal reflux
    disease 85
  plasma levels,
    measurement of 83
  pregnancy 78
  primary care 68
  reversibility of peak
    expiratory flow 14, 15
  therapy-resistant asthma
    86
pregnancy 75–6
  acute exacerbations
    52, 76–7, 78
  aminophylline 79
  β₂-agonists 78
  clinical features 76
  diet 10
  inhaled corticosteroids
    77–8
  intravenous magnesium 79
  leukotriene receptor
    antagonists 38, 39, 81
  management 77
  nicotine replacement
    therapy 28
  oral corticosteroids 78
  theophylline 79
pressurized metered dose
  inhalers (pMDIs) 43
  with spacers 44
prevalence of asthma 2
  age and sex differences
    2–3
  difficult asthma 82
  geographical differences 2

reasons for increase 9–10
temporal trends 3, 4
prevention of exacerbations
  56
primary care 4, 67
  contract 67–9, 72–3
  diagnosis 70
  GP consultations 4
  Quality Outcome
    Framework 67–9, 71,
    72–3
  records 70
  referrals, reasons for 70
  review 69, 71
  staff development 72
prognosis, occupational
  asthma 64
proton pump inhibition 85
provocative dose/
  concentration
  (PD₂₀/PC₂₀)
  bronchial challenge testing
    17, 18
  occupational asthma,
    classical 63
provoking stimuli 12–13
psychological morbidity
  84–5
psychological stress 84, 85
puberty 2
pulsus paradoxus 50

Q

Quality Outcome
  Framework (QOF) 67–9
  limitations 72–3
  review 71
quinolone 29

R

radioimmunoassay test
  (RAST) 18
reactive airways dysfunction
  syndrome (RADS) 59,
  64
  legal issues 65
records, primary care 70
  Quality Outcome
    Framework 69
referral, reasons for 70
refractory (treatment-
  resistant) asthma 82,
  86–7
relaxation techniques,
  pregnancy 77
remodelling of airways 8, 9
renal impairment 38
Reporting of Injuries,
  Diseases and Dangerous
  Occurrences Regulations
  (RIDDOR) 63
respiratory failure 50, 51
restrictive ventilatory
  defects 16

reversible airflow
  obstruction 13
review, primary care 71
  Quality Outcome
    Framework 69
rhinitis, allergic 13, 18–19
  difficult asthma 85
  leukotriene receptor
    antagonists 39
  pharmacological treatment
    of the unified airway 94
  prevalence 3
  primary care 72
RIDDOR 63
rifampicin 40
roflumilast 92
  chemical structure 93

S

salbutamol 13
  acute exacerbations
    52–3, 54, 56
  reversibility of peak
    expiratory flow 14
salmeterol 34
  combination inhalers
    36, 90
  pregnancy 78
Scottish Intercollegiate
  Guidelines Network
  (SIGN) 69, 82
seizures 29
Seretide® 36
sex differences 2–3
short-acting β₂-agonists 33
  occupational asthma,
    classical 63
Singulair™ 38
sinus disease 85
skin prick tests 18
smoking
  bronchial challenge testing
    16
  cessation 27–30
  COPD and asthma,
    overlap between 12
  pregnancy 76, 77
  primary care 69, 71
  reduced plasma
    theophylline 40
spacer devices 43, 44
  adverse effects of
    corticosteroids,
    minimization of 34
  use and maintenance 44
special circumstances
  flying 79–80
  pregnancy 75–9
  underwater diving 79
spirometry 15–16
sputum eosinophilia
  18, 19, 95
staff development, primary
  care 72
steroids see corticosteroids

stress 84, 85
surrogate inflammatory
    biomarkers 18, 19, 95
Symbicort® 36

T

temporal trends 3, 4
terbutaline 33
Th2 cells 5, 6, 7
theophylline 39, 81, 91
    acute exacerbations 54–5
    adverse effects 40
    difficult asthma 83, 87
    plasma levels, measurement
        of 83
    pregnancy 79
therapy-resistant asthma
    82, 86–7
thromboprophylaxis 56
thyrotoxicosis 85
titrating asthma treatment,
    non-invasive methods
    94–5

training, primary care team
    72
tumour necrosis factor
    alpha (TNFα) 94
Turbohaler® 43
type 1 respiratory failure
    50, 51
type 2 respiratory failure
    50, 51

U

ultra long-acting β₂-agonists
    90
underwater diving 79
unified airway, pharmacol-
    ogical treatment of
    the 94

V

verapamil 40
viral causes of exacerbations
    48

vitamin supplementation
    27
vocal cord dysfunction
    82, 83

W

warfarin 38
Westernization, and
    prevalence of asthma
    2, 9
work-aggravated asthma
    59, 64
    legal issues 65

Z

zafirlukast 37
    chemical structure 38
    prescribing and
        pharmacokinetic data
        38
zileuton 37